# Exploring
# the
# Unexplained

# Exploring the Unexplained

**Editor** Kelly Knauer
**Designer** Ellen Fanning
**Picture Editor** Patricia Cadley
**Writer/Research Director** Matthew McCann Fenton
**Copy Editor** Bruce Christopher Carr

## Time Inc. Home Entertainment

**Publisher** Richard Fraiman
**Executive Director, Marketing Services** Carol Pittard
**Director, Retail & Special Sales** Tom Mifsud
**Marketing Director, Branded Businesses** Swati Rao
**Director, New Product Development** Peter Harper
**Financial Director** Steven Sandonato
**Assistant General Counsel** Dasha Smith Dwin
**Prepress Manager** Emily Rabin
**Book Production Manager** Jonathan Polsky
**Marketing Manager** Joy Butts
**Associate Prepress Manager** Anne-Michelle Gallero

**Special thanks to:** Bozena Bannett, Alexandra Bliss, Glenn Buonocore,
Barbara Dudley Davis, Suzanne Janso, Robert Marasco, Brooke McGuire,
Chavaughn Raines, Ilene Schreider, Adriana Tierno, Cornelis Verwaal,
Britney Williams

ISBN: 1-933405-16-3
Library of Congress Control Number: 2006903597

Time Books is a trademark of Time Inc.

We welcome your comments and suggestions about Time Books.
Please write to us at:
Time Books
Attention: Book Editors
PO Box 11016
Des Moines, IA 50336-1016

If you would like to order any of our hardcover Collector's Edition books,
please call us at 1-800-327-6388. (Monday through Friday,
7:00 a.m.- 8:00 p.m. or Saturday, 7:00 a.m.- 6:00 p.m. Central Time).

**Cover photography credits**
**Hardbound edition**
**Front cover:** Alien Head: Chip Simons; Easter Island: Charles & Josette Lenars—Corbis; Shroud of Turin: Veron
Miller—Time Life Pictures; Nazca Lines: Roman Soumar—Corbis; Sphinx: Paul Hardy—Corbis; Stonehenge:
Roger Ressmeyer—Corbis; Hand holding globe: Japack Company—Corbis

**Back cover:** Hypnosis—Ted Lau; Bigfoot—Bettmann Corbis; Ghost—Pictures Inc.—Time Life Pictures;
Twins—Blasius Erlinger—Zefa—Corbis; UFOs—Bettmann Corbis

**Softcover edition**
**Front cover:** Sphinx: Paul Hardy—Corbis; Bigfoot: Bettmann Corbis; Shroud of Turin: Veron Miller—Time Life
Pictures; Ghost: Pictures Inc.—Time Life Pictures; Easter Island: Art Wolfe—Stone—Getty Images; Nazca
Lines: Roman Soumar—Corbis; Alien Head: Chip Simons; Stonehenge: Peter Turner—Getty Images

**Back cover:** Plush Studios—Stone—Getty Images

# Exploring
## the
# Unexplained

## The World's Greatest Marvels, Mysteries and Myths

# TIME

# Contents

## Mysteries of Nature

## Mysteries of Space

## Mind and Matter

## Powers of the Spirit

## A World Beyond

# On Wings of Speculation

A man with wings, soaring above nature and its laws to seek a higher truth: it's an apt metaphor for this book, which explores subjects that transcend our current understanding of our world. From the healing power of prayer to the strange connections between identical twins to researchers probing human senses for which we have yet to find names, this book studies the unexplained: subjects that defy our current comprehension of nature and are thus often relegated to the outskirts of mainstream science.

"Truth is stranger than fiction," Mark Twain once quipped, "because fiction is obliged to stick to possibilities—truth isn't." As was often the case with Twain, this smart-aleck remark was the camouflage that concealed a provocative insight: many times in history the truth has turned out to be a radical departure from what everyone "knew" to be true.

Perhaps that is why important new truths are so often uncovered by fringe figures and outsiders. The location of the city of Troy, long consigned by scholars with smug certainty to the realm of myth, was identified by Heinrich Schliemann, a banker for whom archaeology was a hobby, in the 1870s. The theory of continental drift and plate tectonics, a foundation of our understanding of the planet we live on, was devised by Alfred Wegener, a weatherman whose work was ridiculed for decades by serious geologists.

The search for truth demands rational guidelines, and though some of our subjects may lie on the outer limits of scientific research, we have examined them through science's lens. The scientific method has been mankind's greatest engine of discovery and progress since the Middle Ages, and to say that science is incapable of explaining some of the topics covered in this book is not to condemn its processes, but simply to understand that they work in fits and starts rather than by an orderly timetable.

"Progress occurs only after new empirical evidence becomes so overwhelming that the established orthodoxy just collapses under its weight," reflects Princeton professor Robert Jahn. For two decades Jahn has headed up the Princeton Engineering Anomalies Research laboratory, whose goal is to bring scientific measurement and analysis to reports of paranormal phenomena such as extrasensory perception (ESP), psychokinesis and remote viewing. "It's like a dam breaking," Jahn says. "I believe that we are at a similar threshold at this moment.

But until you reach that point, the old order hangs on and defends itself and fights with every tool at its disposal. For years, we've been finding data that conventional science is not equipped to deal with. So the response from the mainstream scientific community has been to ignore this information whenever possible, and to attack it when it's not possible to ignore it."

Cornell University professor Daryl Bem, another scientist exploring ESP, agrees with Jahn. "There is no other area in psychology, probably anywhere in science, in which a textbook writer would include research done in the 1940s as his most recent data," he says. "Yet that is regarded as acceptable when it comes to psi"—the name academics use for anomalous methods of communication—"because this field is deliberately marginalized."

Not every idea in this book can be taken seriously enough to warrant rigorous scientific investigation, for we've included a few subjects—the search for the yeti, ancient folktales of "undead" vampires—that are a sort of greatest-hits collection of popular notions of the paranormal and occult. It's fascinating to watch fashions in these realms change as inexorably as styles in clothes or entertainment. Our ancestors in the 17th century feared witches and curses; our Victorian forebears were spooked by séances and ghosts; today thousands of people around the planet are obsessed with UFOs and alien abductions.

Writing of the conviction with which some people believe in the Loch Ness Monster, political commentator George F. Will (who does not count himself among the convinced) nonetheless lamented that we live in an age in which "a willingness to construe other persons' beliefs as products of neuroses is widely considered a sign of bravery and learning" and warned that "the world has much to lose from an atrophied capacity for wonder and surprise."

Those who seek a middle path between credulity and cynicism are perhaps best guided by a maxim attributed to Confucius: "To say you know when you know, and to say you do not when you do not, that is knowledge." Guided by the injunction never to say no when we should say we don't know, we have attempted in this book to restore some of the sense of wonder and surprise to our world.

—Matthew McCann Fenton

# MYSTERIES
## OF THE PAST

"It is curious to note the old sea-margins of human thought. Each subsiding century reveals some new mystery; we build where monsters used to hide themselves."

—Henry Wadsworth Longfellow

# NO DECLINE, ALL FALL

Atlantis, the lost continent! Surely these are among the most evocative words in the language, conjuring up visions of ancient triremes, magical crystals and vanished arts and sciences while offering the satisfying notion of an entire classical civilization hurtled into oblivion, pillar by pillar, in a single cataclysmic natural disaster. In short, Atlantis is Pompeii on steroids.

From the days of the ancient Greeks to modern times, tales of this fallen empire have been a tabula rasa onto which current popular fantasies can be projected. Victorian poets made rhymes about Atlantis; Pre-Raphaelite artists painted it; American seer Edgar Cayce visited it in visions. Nazis claimed to share bloodlines with Atlanteans, while folksinger Donovan made Atlantis into a hippy anthem, not long after a hilariously cheesy Hollywood movie depicted the lost

continent as a depraved empire in which berserk scientists armed with killer crystals create a subrace of donkey-eared slaves.

Yet this colossal fictional edifice of bygone grandeur and disaster has been erected upon slender reeds. The tale of Atlantis was first related by Plato. In two dialogues, *Timaeus* and *Critias*, written circa 360 B.C., the Athenian philosopher describes Atlantis as an advanced civilization occupying an island "within the pillars of Hercules," which most scholars believe is a reference to the Strait of Gibraltar. At the center of the island, enclosed within three moats, was a great palace. The Atlanteans conquered Egypt and other lands, Plato tells us, until they were halted by the valiant ancestors of the Athenians. Then, just as the kingdom's power was challenged, "there occurred violent earthquakes and floods; and in a single day and night of misfortune ... Atlantis ... disappeared into the depths of the sea."

To modern ears, this tale of destruction is eerily familiar: the deadly Indian Ocean tsunami of Dec. 26, 2004, reminds us of nature's devastating power. But is Plato's tale—which he claimed occurred 9,000 years before he set it down—based on fact? Or is it merely a folk tale based on secondhand legends of past natural disasters? And if Atlantis was a real place, where was it? The list of suggested locations rivals the manifest at an international airport: the lost continent has been confidently placed in Antarctica, the Caribbean, Indonesia, the Black Sea, the Azores, Scandinavia and Ireland.

Few scholars believe that Atlantis may have been located in the Atlantic Ocean; most place it within the Mediterranean Sea. The kingdom's spectacular demise has led some to propose that its story

is a recollection of the massive eruption of the volcanic island of Thera, now known as Santorini. Some scholars believe this event may have helped destroy the advanced Minoan civilization on Crete, a culture rich in arts, sciences and trade, the memories of which could have inspired Plato's tale. The date of the eruption of Thera is currently much debated, but it is generally assigned to the period between 1650 and 1450 B.C. That is much more recent than Plato's estimate, but in the staggering fall of the Minoan kingdom, we can glimpse the outlines of Atlantis, shimmering across the centuries.

**ATLANTIS?** The island of Santorini (Thera) is the lip of an ancient volcanic caldera. Greek archaeologist Spyridon Marinatos excavated the ruins of an ancient Minoan port on the island and first proposed in 1939 that Santorini was Atlantis. Inset, an 1866 illustrator imagines Thera's eruption.

# SUN-STRUCK TOMB

■ Care to experience the Stone Age at first hand? Join the lucky few who walk into the mysterious mound of earth and quartz called Newgrange, located some 30 miles north of Dublin, Ireland, on the morning of Dec. 21, the winter solstice. As the sun rises on this shortest day of the year, its rays probe the same 60-ft. passage you have taken to the interior of the mound, illuminating its central chamber for about 17 minutes.

Newgrange is one of the oldest buildings made by human hands that we can stand inside today. Believed to have been constructed around 3200 B.C., it is seven centuries older than the pyramids of Egypt, and—as the locals happily boast—at least 1,000 years older than Britain's Stonehenge. Scientists describe this kidney-shaped ruin as a chamber tomb, built to house the remains of a notable person or persons. Such tombs are common to many different ancient cultures; they can be found in Greece, Iran, Malta, Egypt and Mexico. Newgrange is one of the most dramatic of these tombs; in its cruciform central chamber, giant stones support a ceiling that soars 20 ft. over the floor. The mound itself is encircled by 12 large standing stones; it is believed that some 35 similar stones once completely surrounded the site.

Newgrange is only one of a series of such Neolithic burial chambers that lie along the Boyne River in Ireland. The entire complex, called the Brù na Boínne (Palace on the Boyne), includes other passage graves at Knowth and Dowth, as well as standing stones and henges that are similar to, if less impressive than, those familiar from Stonehenge. The 78-acre Brù na Boínne is a UNESCO World Heritage Site, protected by the United Nations. The structure, in ruins and with its ceiling fallen, lay hidden for centuries until it was discovered in 1699 by road builders seeking stone. The complex was extensively reconstructed in the 1970s, using blinding-white original quartz stones found at the site.

The mysteries of Newgrange are many: we know too little about the people who built it, what they believed and whom they considered worthy of the honor of burial within it. Was its central chamber reserved for kings, nobles or priests? And what is the significance of the labyrinth-like spirals that decorate the site? Even more intriguing to scientists is the knowledge required to create such structures; scientists estimate that using Stone Age technology, the building of Newgrange would have required the labor of 300 men working for 20 years. Whether these workers were slaves pressed into service or the faithful, honored to serve, we may never know. However, if you are lucky enough to witness the sun rise on winter-solstice morning at New-grange, you will be among a select few: in 2005, nearly 27,000 people entered a lottery to witness this ancient congruence; 100 were chosen.

**MAZES** A triple spiral design 12 in. in diameter adorns a stone inside the main chamber, below; a large entrance stone also bears the motif. At right, the passage to the central chamber

the periods during which Stonehenge was built. Over the centuries, some Britons have believed Stonehenge was a sacred site of burial for a race of vanished kings. Others claimed it was a temple dedicated to the worship of pagan earth deities. Still others supposed it was built by Merlin the Magician. In recent decades, some have argued that it is an artifact of an advanced extraterrestrial civilization. Today many scientists subscribe to an explanation almost as marvelous: this fabled ruin, they say, served the ancients as a complex astronomical calendar.

The most famous misconception lives on and dates back to 16th century British antiquarians, who believed Stonehenge was a temple sacred to the Druids, the priests of the Celtic civilization that flourished in Western Europe at the time of the Roman Empire. The Druids were pagans: they believed in natural gods and practiced sympathetic magic and soothsaying. Generations of Britons fell in love with Stonehenge's so-called Druid heritage: Romantic poets extolled the ruins; Victorian imperialists touted them as a sign of British endurance and stolidity; 1960s hippies grooved on them and donned neopagan robes to hold annual midsummer rites at the site. The annual gathering of Druid wannabes here on the summer solstice began to take on the aspects of a rock festival, culminating in a semifarcical "Battle of the Beanfield" in 1985, when a convoy of "New Age Travelers" battled British bobbies determined to keep them from over-running the site. Today authorities have severely restricted access to the ruins, to the relief of paleontologists.

In reality, there is no connection between the Druids and this site, for Stonehenge is far older and far more mysterious than the pagan sorcerers who fought the Roman Empire. Today, paleontologists

discover them in 1666. There are no real ruins of the second stage of the site, Stonehenge 2, but postholes reveal that a large timbered structure once stood here; human remains, evidence of cremations, indicate it was used as a funeral site.

Stonehenge 3 is the ruin we see today, featuring 30 enormous stones arranged in a vast circle. Many of them consist of two large standing stones supporting a horizontal pediment stone. Scientists call these structures megaliths, and they marvel at one of the great mysteries of Stonehenge: how builders with no knowledge of the wheel managed to convey the huge, 13.5-ft.-high stones that form them from a quarry located 24 miles to the north. A smaller, older horseshoe of blue-tinged stones inside the main circle has been traced to an even more remote site in Wales, 155 miles away.

Stone Age peoples were sun worshippers, and Stonehenge is aligned to the life-giving star. On a midsummer morning, at dawn on the summer solstice, the sun rises close to the Heel Stone, a marker just outside the circle. Midwinter sunset occurs at the same point. Stonehenge, it seems, was a Stone Age cosmic calendar—or so argued astronomer Gerald Hawkins in his influential 1963 book, *Stonehenge Decoded*. Hawkins found many other astronomical relationships at the site and claimed that Stonehenge was aligned to predict solar eclipses. Many of Hawkins' conjectures have since been questioned, but few scientists doubt that his central conclusion is correct: Stonehenge, like today's most modern telescopes, is our distant ancestors' attempt to see through the veil of the sky—and understand the heavens above.

BIRD'S-EYE VIEW The aerial photograph at bottom left clearly shows many of the 56 "Aubrey holes" near the earthen bunker that encircles the ruins

9

# POINTS TO PIERCE THE HEAVENS

Pyramids exert a peculiar hold on the human imagination. Hilltops were among the first sacred locations in the landscape that early man believed had been given to him by the gods, and the earliest pyramids — aspirations in stone–may have been attempts to rise above the earthly plane and touch the heavens. The pyramids of Egypt are the tetrahedron templates for structures that can be found in almost every culture. The pyramids of the Maya in Central America share similar geometries with those of the ancient Egyptians, a point that continues to intrigue scientists.

Man is everywhere a monument builder, and pyramids were a safe starting point for people beginning to learn mathematics and engineering. As early civilizations mastered technology, rounded mounds of earth became angular piles of stone. It is difficult to build a pyramid that is structurally unsound, which explains why so many of them have survived thousands of years.

The pyramids of Egypt, which were built over a span extending roughly from 2750 to 1525 B.C., remain founts of mystery. Archaeologists still can't explain how the Egyptians were able to create an almost perfectly level base for the Great Pyramid of Cheops, right center, or align it to within a fraction of a degree of true north. The tools that ancient engineers used to cut hard stone, like granite, have never been found. The methods they used to raise giant stone blocks hundreds of feet in the air are also lost to history. Scientists assume that a gigantic system of temporary ramps was built around the pyramid as it was being erected, but no trace of such a structure has been detected. Nor do we know why the two air shafts that emerge from the building's north and south walls were aligned to point to particular stars.

Indeed, even 4,500 years after it was built, we don't know much about the interior of the Great Pyramid itself. In 2003, a robotic camera was inserted through a small hole drilled in a newly discovered door. On the other side, scientists were hoping to find one of several chambers that Egyptian texts hint at, although they have never been found. Instead, they found ... another door.

Our knowledge of the pyramids continues to evolve. For centuries, scholars took the word of Greek historian Herodotus that the pyramids at Giza were built by an army of 100,000 slaves, laboring for more than a century. But recently uncovered archaeological evidence suggests that the project took only about 20 years to complete and was the work of some 20,000 laborers—most of whom were volunteers contributing a prestigious form of national service for a few months at a time, primarily during the Nile's flood season, when there was little work for farmers.

Nature abhors a vacuum: where facts are few, fables flourish. Although the pyramids were clearly erected as royal tombs and temples, their origin and function have inspired fanciful hypotheses from the moment Egypt's classical civilization declined. Among the wilder notions: the pyramids were constructed under the guidance of extraterrestrials or by an ancient civilization of superhuman beings.

Yet the down-to-earth mysteries of pyramids are so tantalizing, they don't require alien intervention to intrigue us. For example, the mathematical ratio between the height of the Great Pyramid of Cheops and its base suggests that the ancient Egyptians had a rough idea of the value of pi. If true, this finding would rewrite our knowledge of the history of science. Alas, there is no irrefutable evidence that the ratio's occurrence is anything more than a coincidence.

The pyramids are marvelous indeed. But if you visit Egypt bearing theories that aliens designed and built them, rather than the forebears of modern-day Egyptians, don't be surprised if English-speaking locals describe you with the term they have coined for overly credulous tourists: pyramidiots.

SURVIVOR **The Great Pyramid of Cheops at Giza, center, is believed to date from 2500 B.C. It was damaged by an earthquake in A.D. 1301, dislodging its smooth casing stones. Its current height is 455 ft.**

# JINX OF THE SPHINX

Poised at the dawn of recorded history, the ancient Egyptians and their culture have fascinated mankind down through the ages. The Egyptians' beliefs and gods, their arts and sciences, their massive building projects, their mummification of bodies in preparation for the afterlife — all these elements coalesce to make the ancient kingdom of the Nile a magnet for wonder

**THE SPHINX:** A mythical creature with the head of a man and the body of a lion, the sphinx was a common icon in Egypt. The Great Sphinx of Giza, at right, is the most splendid and familiar of the breed. Facing east with a temple between its paws, it is some 260 ft. long and 65 ft. high. Its head is said to be modeled after that of the Pharaoh Khafra, who ruled from 2558 to 2532 B.C.; some scholars suspect it may be even older. The Greeks adopted the beast, making it a sign of ill omen. The Great Sphinx may well be jinxed, but the familiar story that Napoleon's soldiers blew its nose off while firing cannons in target practice is not true. The structure may have been vandalized by Islamic fanatics in the 14th century. Some recent writers have speculated that the Sphinx is some 10,500 years old, and that it is oriented to the constellations; scientists are unconvinced.

**AFTERLIFE JOURNEYS:** Remote in time and alien in belief, Egypt's culture has attracted speculation and pseudoscience for centuries. Like many of mankind's earliest major structures, pyramids, tombs and the passageways within them are in some cases oriented to the positions of the stars or the movement of the sun. Above is a passageway in the funerary chamber of the Pharaoh Ramses VI, in the Valley of the Kings at Luxor. The Egyptians believed in life after death, as seen in the detail from the Papyrus of Ani (circa 1240 B.C.), which shows the winged Ba, a soul or spirit through which the dead would someday join the afterlife, leaving Ani's mummy.

**TUT'S CURSE:** Since British archaeologist Howard Carter first entered the vault where the sarcophagus of the boy pharaoh Tutankhamen, right, reposed in 1922, "King Tut" has fascinated the world.

Above, a 2005 reconstruction of Tut's face is based on CT scans of his mummy. When the expedition's sponsor, Lord Carnarvon, died shortly after the find, rumors arose of a supposed "curse of King Tut's tomb." But tales of legions of scientists dying after being in the vault are pure fiction.

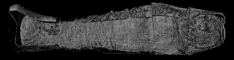

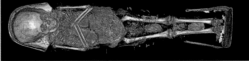

**MUMMIES:** Believing the spirit would rejoin the body in the afterlife, the Egyptians removed many of the body's organs, then covered it with natron, a salt, to speed dehydration. The corpse was then shrouded in strips of linen. Animals were also mummified. Arab scholars were the first to believe that mummies possessed magical, medicinal powers. Curses were placed on the rich tombs of royal mummies in Egypt, to ward off grave robbing—a boon to Hollywood scriptwriters, if not a deterrent to crime.

Above, a beaded faience covers the face of a mummy discovered in March 2005. The images below it are CT scans showing different views of the 2,000-year-old mummified body of a 4- to 6-year-old girl preserved in its linen wrappings.

# MISTS OF THE PAST

ACCOUNTS OF INHALING FUMES THAT ENGENDER TRANCES MAY
SOUND LIKE MUMBO-JUMBO (OR REEFER MADNESS) TO MODERN EARS

For centuries devout Greeks tramped up the side of Mount Parnassus, 100 miles northwest of Athens, to consult the most renowned soothsayer of the ancient world, the Oracle at Delphi. Here, at a spectacular site perched on a steep slope, the gods revealed the future. Their medium, as the historian Plutarch tells us, was a young woman who sat in a chair over a fissure in the rocks, inhaling sweet-smelling fumes emitted from the ground that put her into a euphoric trance. Under this influence she would speak in tongues; priests would later interpret her remarks. The savvy initiates in charge of the rites, eager to please clients, were practiced in ambiguity. When Croesus of Lydia asked his fate if he invaded Persia, he was told, "If Croesus crosses the Halys [River], a great empire will be destroyed."

No doubt the priests exhaled when Croesus was trounced ... destroying his own empire.

Accounts of inhaling fumes that engender trances may sound like mumbo-jumbo (or reefer madness) to modern ears. Yet when geologists from two U.S. universities explored the sacred site in the 1990s, they supported Plutarch. In the August 2001 issue of *Geology*, Jelle Z. de Boer and his team noted that two tectonic fault lines lie beneath the site, from which ethylene gas may have issued in bygone days — and sweet-smelling ethylene is known to produce euphoric hallucinations. For once, modern science helped confirm ancient legends, rather than shatter them.

**FOG** **Left, Delphi today. Above, a Victorian artist's view of the scene. An early Oracle was known as Sibyl, and later mediums adopted that name; it is now used as a generic term for a prophet**

# ALTERNATE HISTORIES

The world's museums and rare-book libraries are home to a number of artifacts that provide tantalizing glimpses of alternate storylines for mankind. Runestones and maps suggest Vikings explored America centuries before Columbus, while other curious objects seem to project modern-day technology into the distant past. Each item on these pages is the subject of vigorous debate

**PRE-COLOMBIAN PLANE:** The delta-winged object at right, crafted of gold, was found in Central America and has been dated to A.D. 500 to 800. Some scientists call the tiny piece a zoomorph, saying it is designed to represent an animal, but it bears an obvious resemblance to a 20th century airplane; it even seems to include a pilot's seat. Such an aircraft would have made an ideal vehicle from which to view the famed Nazca lines formed on the high desert plains of Peru.

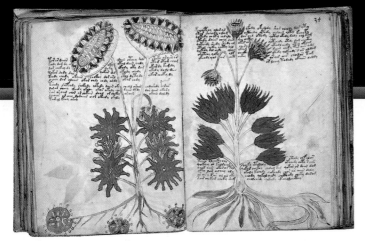

**PIRI REIS MAP:** Made in 1513 by Piri Reis, a Turkish cartographer and mariner, this map, drawn on gazelle skin, was discovered in 1929 in Istanbul. It seems to show part of the coastline of Antarctica, years before that polar continent was first discovered and mapped.

**VOYNICH MANUSCRIPT:** Paging *The Da Vinci Code* author Dan Brown! This mysterious, incomplete book consists of 240 vellum pages filled with illustrations of herbs, plants and the zodiac. Written in a strange script that has defied deciphering by the world's top cryptologists, it has been called the Holy Grail of code-breakers. Believed to date from the 15th or early 16th century, it was bought by incunabulist Wilfrid Voynich in 1912; it is now owned by the Yale University Library.

**FRENCH TOKEN:** How did the circular flying object at left, which might be a refugee from a 20th century account of a "flying saucer," end up on a token minted in France in 1680? Among other past references to UFOs are a 1561 event in Nuremberg, Germany, when many residents reported seeing disks and spheres in the sky; citizens of Basel, Switzerland, saw similar flying machines over their city five years later.

**KENSINGTON RUNESTONE:** The slab of sandstone at left is at the heart of a long-running dispute. Discovered by Swedish-American farmer Olof Ohman in 1898 while he was plowing in Kensington, Minn., the stone is covered with runes recounting a visit to the area by 14th century Scandinavian explorers. Generations of linguists cast doubt on the accuracy of the runes, but in more recent years some scholars have argued that the writing is authentic. The stone remains one of history's most intriguing mysteries.

**VINLAND MAP:** Discovered in 1957 and believed to date from the 15h century, this map of the world shows a land mass titled Vinland, corresponding to today's Greenland. The map claims Vinland was found in the 11th century by Vikings from Scandinavia. Some scholars say the map, now owned by Yale University, is a hoax; the issue is unresolved.

# ONE BRIEF SHINING MOMENT

We all know the tale of King Arthur, Guinevere, Merlin, Lancelot and the Knights of the Round Table. But is the story of Camelot pure fantasy, or does it contain a few shards of truth, however obscured by our ignorance of Britain's Dark Ages, when the saga is set? Much of what we know of Arthur was first set down by a 12th-century Tolkien, Geoffrey of Monmouth. The British monk wrote his popular and highly fanciful account of Camelot six centuries after his subject died—assuming he ever lived in the first place.

Debate has swirled for centuries around the mythic—but perhaps not mythological—figure of King Arthur. The one verifiable historical event to which Arthur can be linked is the Battle of Mount Badon at the end of the 5th century A.D. In this engagement near present-day Bath, the disparate, feuding fiefdoms of Britain united for the first time to defeat, against considerable odds, invading hordes of Saxons from what is now Germany. So momentous was this banding together of the warlords who ruled early England, and so enduringly popular was Geoffrey of Monmouth's retelling of it, that in the 14th century King Edward III founded the Order of the Garter in imitation of Arthur's court. He even held his councils of state around a specially built Round Table. A century later, the Tudor kings of England, among them Henry VIII, sought to bolster their legitimacy by claiming to be descended from Arthur. The mystique of Camelot endures, from Disney films to Broadway musicals to the Kennedy White House.

Many historians were skeptical that Arthur was a historical figure. Then, in 1998, scientists unearthed a broken stone at Tintagel Castle on Britain's Cornish coast, long said to be Arthur's stronghold. The stone bore the Latin inscription *Pater Coliavificit Artognov,* which translates as "Artognou, father of a descendant of Coll, has had this built." Artognou is pronounced "Arthnou," lending credence to theories that the legendary king was real. And as for Coll, you've heard of him as well—remember "Old King Cole"?

TRACES OF CAMELOT Legend says that Tintagel Castle in Cornwall was Arthur's keep. At left is Glastonbury Abbey, also associated with Arthur's reign. Inset: a rendering of the fabled king from a medieval tapestry

19

# POSTCARDS

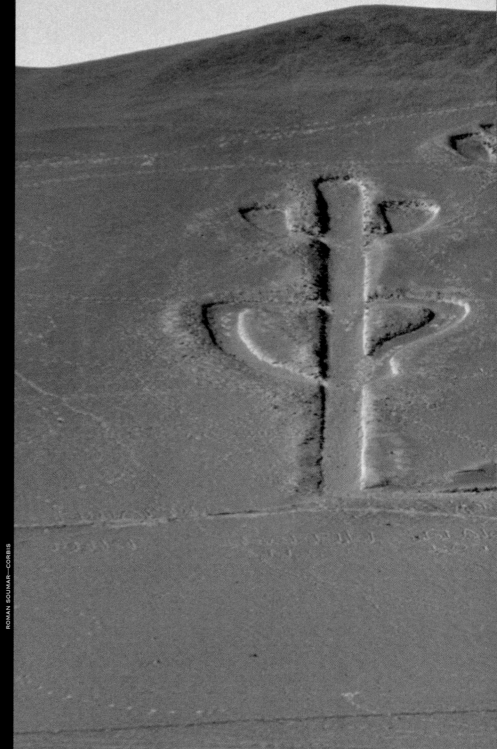

Long before Columbus, long before the Incas, Maya and Aztecs, the people of Peru's vanished Nazca culture created enormous drawings on a desert plain high in the Andes called the Pampa Colorada, some 250 miles south of Lima. If there are miracles here, one is meteorological: the lines have been preserved like new for centuries by the arid high-desert air, the static climate stopping time.

Seen from the ground, the lines are mystifying, their significance unclear. They are indented furrows, where dark stones that cover the ground have been removed to expose lighter soil beneath. Yet seen from the air, the only place from which they can be viewed in their entirety, many of them come into focus, forming a bestiary of curios: a hummingbird, a spiral-tailed monkey, a condor, an owl-headed man. Other drawings form clear geometric shapes: spirals, trapezoids and parallel lines. The animal shapes were created first; scientists date them to 200 B.C. The geometric forms were created some 500 years later. Scientists call the shapes geoglyphs, or earth writings. The mystery they pose is this: Why would people unable to fly create shapes so large they can only be appreciated from a vantage point high in the sky?

Most scientists believe the images were directed not to man's eyes but to those of the gods. Swiss author Erich von Daniken expanded on this point, famously arguing in his 1970 best seller, *Chariots of the Gods,* that the pictograms were messages to alien navigators, and the desert a landing strip for ancient spaceships. Readers loved the notion, but scientists were scornful. One resourceful group in the 1980s sucessfully built and flew a primitive hot-air balloon on the site, hoping to prove that the Nazca people could indeed see the figures from on high.

The lines were protected from harm for decades by German mathematician Maria Reiche, who argued that they served as ancient sky calendars. That theory was firmly refuted by astronomer Gerald Hawkins. Other scientists have proposed that the lines point to ancient underground aquifers, while still others suspect that they were walked by pilgrims during religious rites, visiting simple shrines that vanished long ago. The exact function of these lines remains one of the great unsolved mysteries of the past.

HANDS UP! The shapes cover 400 sq. mi. of desert. This figure, called the Candelabro for obvious reasons, is 800 ft. long. Some think it shows a local hallucinogenic cactus

ROMAN SOUMAR—CORBIS

# BUT FOR WHOSE EYES?

■ WHY WOULD PEOPLE UNABLE TO FLY CREATE VISIONS THAT CAN ONLY BE APPRECIATED FROM HIGH ABOVE GROUND?

# SILENT SENTINELS

"The stone images at first caused us to be struck with astonishment," explorer Jacob Roggeveen wrote in 1722, shortly after he and his fellow Dutch mariners discovered Easter Island, "because we could not comprehend how it was possible that these people, who are devoid of heavy thick timber for making any machines, as well as strong ropes, nevertheless had been able to erect such images, which were fully 30 ft. high and thick in proportion."

Roggeveen was only the first visitor to marvel at the massive, mystifying totems of this island civilization. This 63-sq.-mi. scrap of land—which the Dutch christened for the feast day when they made landfall—seems stranded in the vast Pacific: it lies 2,237 miles west of Chile and 1,290 miles east of the nearest Polynesian isle, Pitcairn Island. Spooked by the island's remoteness (it is the most isolated human outpost on earth) and the harsh desolation of its surface, visitors have long proposed supernatural or extraterrestrial origins for the haunting *moai,* the natives' name for the hundreds of eerie, monolithic statues that dot its hillsides.

The island poses a quartet of questions. Who settled it? Who built the *moai*? What technology did they employ? And what happened to the builders?

In the 20th century, Norwegian marine biologist Thor Heyerdahl insisted, against all evidence, that Easter's inhabitants must have come from South America, rather than Polynesia. And without much evidence whatsoever, Swiss writer Erich von Daniken of *Chariot of the Gods* fame was sure the *moai* had been carved by stranded space travelers who were later rescued.

Other scientists' answers are less exotic—and more disturbing. The landmass its natives call Rapa Nui ("Great Island," in the Polynesian language) emerged from the waves in a series of volcanic eruptions that began some 3 million years ago. Through the ages that followed, the nine-mile-wide island was inhabited only by seabirds and insects. Then, around A.D. 900, Polynesian mariners found it. Located more than two-thirds of the way between the Polynesian islands and South America, Easter Island would mark the eastward limit of Polynesian expansion.

The first settlers, a party perhaps a few dozen strong, came upon a verdant paradise that included a now extinct

variety of palm tree that was the tallest in the world, growing to more than 60 ft., with a trunk that could reach 7 ft. in diameter. These trees provided wood from which to make canoes (fishing supported the population), as well as timber that could be used to slide large pieces of stone. The islanders fashioned rope from palm bark, using it to hoist the statues, the heaviest of which weigh more than 80 tons.

Generations of the island's growing population began carving the *moai* out of volcanic rock around A.D. 1100. The figures appear to have been dedicated to revered ancestors and chiefs, who were worshiped as gods, and were positioned to stand watch over the territories of the squabbling tribes into which the descendants of the island's colonizers were dividing.

But this small, sea-girded land offered no frontier. And its life-supporting palm trees may have numbered no more than 100,000. As the population swelled to an estimated peak of about 15,000 around the year 1500, the need for more fishing boats, more fuel for cooking fires and more timber and rope for transporting and erecting the *moai* led to rapid deforestation.

Once the trees were gone, it was no longer possible to fish or build fires. Farming became untenable because topsoil, no longer sheltered by trees or anchored by roots, blew away in the wind. The inhabitants appear to have continued building their monoliths for as long as they could. Jared Diamond, author of *Collapse: How Societies Choose to Fail or Succeed*, interprets the work as a series of increasingly desperate pleas for help from powerful ancestors. Indeed, mute testimony to the suddenness of the disaster is provided by the *moai* themselves: hundreds of the statues, in various stages of completion, lie inside the volcanic cinder cone where the rock was quarried. The work site gives the appearance of having been abandoned on short notice.

Faced with desperate scarcity, the island's tribes went to war with one another. The conquerors appear to have resorted to cannibalism. By the time Roggeveen arrived, little more than two centuries after the island's glory days, its population had dropped to some 2,000 people, most of whom were living in caves. The survivors could no longer remember who had erected the *moai*, much less how or why.

**WITNESSES** Left, a line of *moai* stands guard over a beach. Inset, statues on a hillside. There are 877 statues on the island; half of them lie unfinished in a volcanic quarry

# MOUNTAINS, MYTHS AND MANDALAS

No human dream is more universal than the longing for a paradise on earth, a place free of the ravages of time and disease, where the best in nature flourishes while the worst is forbidden to enter. By definition, such magical lands can't be near at hand; they must be remote and inaccessible, destinations to be reached by pilgrimage or a heroic journey. Ancient Tibetan Buddhist texts spoke of just such a kingdom, where wise kings blessed with long life spans await the day when they will take power over the world, ushering in a golden age of peace and justice. This mythical kingdom was called Shambala. Its location— known only to a few initiates—was reputed to be in northern India ... or in Xinjiang province in western China ... or even near the Gobi

Desert. Said to be enclosed by a double ring of snow-capped mountains, the fabled vale of Shambala resembled a mandala, Buddhism's circular symbol of the unity of all creation.

Known only to a few European Asia enthusiasts in the 19th century, the myth of Shambala was popularized in the 20th century by the famous Russian mystic and founder of Theosophy, Madame Blavatsky, who claimed she received telepathic messages from the mystic valley. Then, with interest in Shambala growing, the myth was essentially hijacked by British novelist James Hilton, whose 1933 best seller *Lost Horizon* gave Shambala a new name: Shangri-la.

In Hilton's tale, a party of Europeans is evacuated by plane from

A PLACE FREE OF THE RAVAGES OF TIME AND DISEASE, WHERE THE BEST
IN NATURE FLOURISHES AND THE WORST IS FORBIDDEN TO ENTER

Central Asia just as a nightmarish war erupts. But the plane crashes in a valley deep within the then unexplored country of Tibet. Here they encounter a community of monks who seemingly live forever and stand guard over the accumulated wisdom of mankind. Hilton transformed the name by fusing that of a remote pass near Mount Everest discovered by explorer George Mallory in the 1920s (*Changri*) with the Tibetan word for such passes (*la*).

Published just as Adolf Hitler came to power in Germany, Hilton's book tapped into deep yearnings for a modern utopia, and the exotic name Shangri-la soon adorned restaurants, hotels and clubs around the world, including President Franklin D. Roosevelt's new hideaway in the Catoctin Mountains outside Washington. A later President

Dwight Eisenhower, didn't share F.D.R.'s romanticism; he renamed the retreat after his grandson: Camp David.

Sadly, the land where the legend of Shambala was born, Tibet, has been occupied by China since 1949. Today Beijing hasn't lost its taste for conquest, although its idea of power seems to be drawn more from the cash register than the barrel of a gun. In 2002 the government tried to cash in on the ancient mythical land of Tibetan lamas by renaming the western town of Zhongdian as Shangri-la. Even so, the words Hilton wrote in 1933 are truer than ever today: "You will not find Shangri-la marked on any map."

RETREAT **Above, temples in Xinjiang province, one site of the fabled land of Shambala, pictured within twin mountain ranges in the mandala at left**

# STEEPED IN MYSTERY

Like Newgrange and Giza, Stonehenge and Delphi, the sacred sites of vanished cultures inspire endless speculation. Why, for example, did the pyramid form spread so widely across the ancient world? Were pre-Columbian Americans influenced by the work of the Egyptians—or is the four-sided tetrahedron a universal, primal image? The questions far outnumber the answers

**KAILASA:** One of the world's most astonishing structures, this great complex, sacred to Hindus, was not built but carved, excavated out of solid rock. Located in Ellora, India, the main temple, 98 ft. high, was modeled after the peak of Mount Kailasa in the Himalayas. The building of the complex, scientists estimate, took place around A.D. 750 and required more than 100 years of labor

**TEOTIHUACAN:** Pyramids are found across the ancient world, from Egypt and the Middle East to the Americas. But why did the shape cast such a spell? Right, the Temple of the Moon is only one of a magnificent complex of pyramids and temples at Teotihuacán in Mexico. The sacred city dates to 300 B.C.; its builders are unknown.

**SACSAYHUAMAN:** Peru's Machu Picchu is the most familiar example of the great works of pre-Columbian Americans, but it is only one of many. When Spanish conquistadors first beheld Sacsayhuaman, left, north of Cuzco, they marveled at its advanced technology: here giant stones of enormous weight have been hewn to fit tightly together, needing no mortar. Along with the Inca's capital city of Cuzco and the Tullumayo River, this site forms an enormous geoglyph, or earth drawing, in the shape of a puma, the sacred totem of the Incas.

**DJOSER:** At right is the Pyramid of Djoser, the first known step pyramid built in Egypt—or anywhere else. Such structures are precursors of the more technically complex slope-sided pyramids of later centuries. Scientists believe the Egyptians moved from this early version to the more advanced design in only a century or two. Djoser's pyramid is similar to the Mesopotamian ziggurat, the model for the Old Testament's Tower of Babel, an enduring symbol of man's hopes and follies.

Joseph Campbell, the scholar of mythology, suggested the design of such buildings traveled from the Middle East to India and China, then—somehow—crossed the ocean to influence prehistoric Americans.

# mysteries of
## nature

# abominable snow job?

When Alexander the Great invaded India in 326 B.C., he was intrigued by tales of a local ape that was taller than a man, had no tail and walked upright. Alexander commanded that one be brought before him but was was told the animals lived only near the tops of remote mountains. Four centuries later, the Roman historian Pliny the Elder wrote of "creatures … with human-like bodies [that] can run on both four feet and two," that lived "in the mountains … east of India."

The peoples of Asia have long believed in a beast more human than any other animal yet still wild. The creature has many names: he is the nyalmo in northern India, the chemo in Nepal, the yeti in Tibet, the yeren in China, the almas in Mongolia, the mawa in Malaysia. All the names, most of which incorporate words meaning man, wild, mountain or snow, describe a 7-to-10-ft.-tall primate, covered head to foot with shaggy hair, walking erect, living in remote regions (usually at high altitudes), shy of human contact but dangerous if cornered or provoked.

The most common signs of the yeti are his large footprints, left in snow or mud, and his piercing call— unnerving, mournful shrieks, usually heard at night, that carry across great distances, even in blizzards. Natives say the yeti devours yaks and sheep, which are sometimes found torn to pieces. Stories of supposed yeti harm to humans are often attempts to account for the unexplained disappearance of herdsmen, sans evidence.

For Western explorers, the search for the yeti offers a chance to make reputations, either through confirming the stories (by killing or capturing one of the creatures) or disproving them. Sir Edmund Hillary, the New Zealander who first conquered Mount Everest in 1953, returned to the Himalayas in 1960, resolved to demystify the monster. After a fruitless 10-month hunt, he concluded that it was all "a fascinating fairy tale, born of the rare and frightening view of strange animals, molded by superstition, and enthusiastically nurtured by western expeditions." In the 1980s, Johns Hopkins University researcher Daniel Taylor-Ide ascribed most sightings and other evidence to a large species of indigenous bear. In the year 2000, ace Alpine mountaineer Reinhold Messner also pronounced, after a years-long inquiry, that the yeti was ursine, rather than simian.

Amid the fray, locals remain calm. In 1961, when French scholars told Himalayan village elder Khunjo Chumbi they believed the yeti was a hoax, he replied, "In Nepal we have neither giraffes nor kangaroos, so we know nothing about them. In France, there are no yetis, so I sympathize with your ignorance."

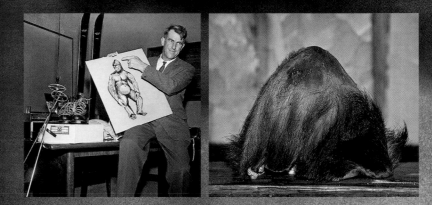

**ELUSIVE BEAST** Above left, Sir Edmund Hillary holds a hypothetical sketch of a yeti during his 1960 expedition. Right, a "yeti skull" in a Tibetan monastery turned out to be that of a goat. The two large pictures show mysterious tracks in the snow located during the Hillary expedition; he concluded they were made by a bear. Some scientists have proposed the yeti may be an undiscovered descendant of *Gigantopithecus*, a large hominid that lived in Asia around 300,000 years ago

# the lady of the loch

For as long as humans living in the Highlands of Scotland have left written records, stories have persisted of giant creatures lurking in the murky depths of the region's peat-darkened lakes. The Picts, a fierce tribal people subdued by the Romans in the 1st century A.D., left many stone carvings of local animals. All are easily identifiable by modern scholars, except for one: it shows a large beast with an elongated neck, small head and long tail, as well as a thick trunk whose legs ended in flippers, rather than feet.

Five centuries later, when St. Columba brought Christianity to Scotland, he is said to have awed the Picts by subduing a sea monster on the River Ness. According to an account written a century later, Columba "raised his holy hand ... and, invoking the name of God, formed the saving sign of the cross in the air, and commanded the ferocious monster, saying, 'Thou shalt go no further ...' Then at the voice of the saint, the monster was terrified, and fled more quickly than if it had been pulled back with ropes." The amazed locals quickly converted to Christianity.

The Loch Ness Monster is named for Scotland's most voluminous lake, which holds more fresh water than can found in England and Wales combined; locals have long called her Nessie for short. She became a 20th century obsession in 1933, when game hunter Marmaduke Wetherell, who had been hired by a British tabloid newspaper eager to boost sales, "discovered" the footprints of a giant animal in the mud by the side of the lake. Plaster casts of these tracks were shipped off to London's Natural History Museum, where they were found to have been made by a stuffed hippopotamus foot, then fashionable for umbrella stands and ashtrays.

In the months it took researchers to debunk the footprints, Wetherell ensured that events on the Nessie beat stayed hot. His son and stepson faked the classic photo of the monster at right, using a toy submarine fitted with a toy sea-serpent head as a stand-in for the monster. They gave the undeveloped photo to Robert Wilson, an eminent London gynecologist interested in the case, who had it developed and released it to a newspaper in Scotland as his own. The image persuaded generations of Nessie hunters that their prey was alive, if elusive.

It wasn't until 1994, 61 years after the photo was first printed, that two investigators coaxed a deathbed confession from Wetherell's stepson. Wilson, front man for the hoax, either believed the photo was real or thought the prank would only reach a local audience rather than an international one. He once said there was room for "slight doubt" about the photo's authenticity.

Tales of Nessie endure, for she has become a sort of folk hero.

Local merchants have an especially soft spot for the beast: imaginary or not, she pumps a very real $40 million into the region's economy each year.

In recent decades, numerous sonar scans of the loch have failed to find Nessie. However, several scans have found "anomalies" that might be large schools of salmon or might be something else. In 2003, an intact specimen of four fossilized giant vertebrae was found on the shores of the loch. The bones were later identified as those of a plesiosaur, an ancient sea reptile that had a small head, elongated neck and tail and four paddle-like flippers for limbs.

in 2003 an intact specimen of four fossilized giant vertebrae was found on the shores of loch ness. the bones were later identified as those of a plesiosaur

Scientists cannot explain how the fossil got there. Many sightings of the Loch Ness Monster sound uncannily like descriptions of a plesiosaur—including its length of about 35 ft., tallying with accounts of Nessie. But there are serious problems with proposing that Nessie is—or was—a plesiosaur. Those big reptiles lived in the oceans, not fresh water; they were cold-blooded animals adapted to a subtropical temperatures—meaning they probably could not survive the frigid depths of the loch. And then there's the dating problem: the last plesiosaurs lived around 65 million years ago, but the loch itself was formed at the end of the last Ice Age and is

only about 10,000 years old. Scientists say chances the specimen originated where it was found are slim; it may have been deposited by a glacier—or planted to ensure the saga of Nessie lives on.

So the debate continues, as happy tourists flock to the loch. Perhaps the last word belongs to G.K. Chesterton, the British intellectual of the early 20th century, who wrote, "Many a man has been hanged on less evidence than there is for the Loch Ness Monster."

FRAUD! The image above ranks near the top among the most famous photo hoaxes in history. One of its perpetrators confirmed it was a fake in a deathbed confession six decades after it was forged—on April Fool's Day, 1933

Bigfoot, the oversized, shaggy-haired primate whose natural habitat long seemed to be the pages of supermarket tabloids, is attracting something other than dismissive sneers from scientists

# prints of a fellow?

"I'm sure that they exist," said Jane Goodall, one of the world's leading primatologists, about the giant ape known as "Bigfoot" in 2002. Surprised? Yes, Bigfoot, the oversized, shaggy-haired primate whose natural habitat long seemed to be the pages of supermarket tabloids and late-night TV shlockumentaries, is attracting something other than dismissive sneers from the academic community. Goodall is one of a growing chorus of respected scientists who say the matter is worth serious study. George Schaller, director of science at the Wildlife Conservation Society, and Conservation International primatologist Russell Mittermier (who has discovered five new species of primates in the past 10 years) are among numerous scientists who have called for more investigation into the existence of Bigfoot.

Why? Zoologists point to the raft of species once believed mythical or extinct whose existence has been confirmed in modern times: the giant squid, mountain gorilla, giant panda, okapi, coelacanth and (we hope) ivory-billed woodpecker. The "living fossil" squirrel, once known only through remains, was found thriving in Laos in March 2006.

Then there's the specific evidence. Almost every known group of Native American languages contains a word for a giant ape, while archaeological digs in the U.S. West have uncovered rock carvings of a large primate—especially fascinating since science is unaware of any large monkeys being native to North America. How could so many different cultures, most of which had no contact with one another, have independently imagined a similar unusual critter?

There are recorded sightings of Bigfoot going back to the 1820s, with more than 2,500 reports since 1900. And more recently, there have been some intriguing forensic clues. The best of them is the Skookum Cast, a plaster imprint of the impression left by a large animal in a muddy Mount St. Helens meadow in 2000. When amateur Bigfoot seekers who had baited the area with a pile of fruit returned, they found that whatever had taken their stash had a large forearm, a hairy thigh, protruding buttocks and what may be an Achilles tendon. Skeptics say that if the cast is a forgery, it was done by experts.

PHOTO OP? Left, the film taken by Roger Patterson and Robert Gimlin in Northern California in 1967 is one of the most familiar images of Bigfoot. Skeptics say it's a human in a costume. Above, Dale Wallace holds the molds his father used to fake footprints

Now for the bad news. Some of the most familiar evidence for the big fellow's existence *is* false. In 2003 the adult children of Ray Wallace, whose 1958 "discovery" of footprints apparently left by an enormous ape in Washington State made headlines, revealed that it had all been a prank hatched by their late father. In 2004, Bob Heironimus, a retired Pepsi bottler, claimed to have climbed into a giant gorilla costume to make the famed movie of Bigfoot at left; others involved with this film still maintain that it is real.

Skeptics also point to the "habeas corpus" test: no one has ever found the remains (contemporary or fossilized) of such a creature, even though fossils turn up regularly for mammoths, dinosaurs and other creatures that disappeared from North America eons ago.

Even so, Schaller—who remains unconvinced but is also unwilling to write off Bigfoot's existence—says, "There have been so many sightings over the years. Even if you throw out 95% of them, there ought to be some explanation for the rest. The same goes for some of these tracks. I think a hard-eyed look is absolutely essential."

# bestiary of illusions

Once upon a time, millions believed that the creatures on these pages existed; mythical or not, they embody mankind's wishes, fears and urges. Some, like fairies, are figures from folktales. Some, like the dragon and unicorn, are emblems of power or purity. And some, like the golem and the phoenix, are archetypes that express our deepest impulses: to create life or renew it eternally

**THE PHOENIX:** The Egyptians gave us this imaginary creature that lives for centuries, builds a pyre and burns into ash, then forms again. An emblem of the soul's renewal, the mythical fire-bird lives on in many cultures, from *Harry Potter* books to this statue , which presides over the rebirth of bombed Hiroshima.

**THE GOLEM:** In Jewish mystical tradition, the golem is a being made of dust or mud, animated by religious words or spells. The most famed golem, seen in the statue at right, is said to have been created by a 16h century rabbi, the Maharal of Prague; it protected the Jews of the Prague ghetto from anti-Semites.

**THE DRAGON:** Dragons have soared through men's imaginations for centuries; they are popular in many cultures, although the Oriental version often lacks wings and is benevolent, while the ornery European critter flies around belching flame and distressing damsels. Dragons are kin to snakes, which always symbolize evil. Quetzalcoatl, the dragon-serpent of Mesoamerican lore, was feathered. In a popular medieval tale, St. George rescued a maiden by slaying a dragon, as illustrated above by Florentine painter Paolo Uccello.

**THE "LITTLE PEOPLE":** Our world would be a sadder place without fairies, elves, dwarfs, leprechauns and the scores of other sprites that populate the folktales of almost every culture. Some scientists suspect that trolls and dwarfs may reflect prehistoric memories of the days when *Cro magnon* men and Neanderthals lived side by side. Modern Icelanders widely believe in local spirits; they refer to patterns in moss as "fairy rings" and build roads to detour around fairy habitats.

**THE UNICORN:** The ancient Greeks and Romans, perhaps stimulated by tales of the rhinoceros and samples of the Arctic narwhal's single horn, believed that unicorns existed. By medieval times, unicorns were emblems of purity: they were attracted to virgins, and their horns were viewed as antidotes to all kinds of poisons. Below, a scene from the stunning 15th century tapestry series *The Hunt of the Unicorn*.

**THE WEREWOLF:** Shape shifters, humans who turn into animals, are present in many folk cultures. The werewolf was known to the Greeks and Romans, but our version, which changes form at the full moon and can be killed by a silver bullet, derives from Nordic and Germanic tales.

# stargazing's twilight

Astrology is the single most influential pseudoscience in human history. Its influence is everywhere, from the ancient pyramids of Egypt to the plays of Shakespeare to Ronald Reagan's White House. Across the globe, millions of people who consider themselves immune to superstition wouldn't think of starting their day without consulting a newspaper or online horoscope. Battles have been won and lost and children have been conceived based on the alignment of the stars, and in modern-day India, wedding planners complain that too many nuptials are scheduled for a small number of days—those identified as auspicious by the heavens.

Yet mainstream scientists, without exception, say astrology is utterly bogus, and even its proponents struggle to explain how the position of celestial bodies at our birth could possibly influence our personalities, much less our destinies. Yet who among us has not consulted a horoscope, only to find that our character traits reflect precisely the qualities put forth by astrologers: tidy Virgo, bull-headed Taurus, sexy Scorpio, unpredictable Gemini.

The notion that our fate may be tangled up in the stars is present in almost all human cultures and dates from mankind's earliest days: the pyramids, chamber tombs and ancient megaliths of ancient history were built to align with the heavens. Yet as science has replaced superstition in man's affairs, astrology's influence has, so to speak, entered retrograde. In its first manifestation, men believed the stars and planets played a direct role in human affairs, and the first astrologers were priest-magicians of enormous power. By the Middle Ages, astrologers no longer believed the stars controlled our destinies but thought signs and portents involving human affairs could be read in the heavens. Today, the powers claimed for astrology are much diminished, and the discipline is valued by most of its users for the insights it is believed to offer into personality types.

Yet astrology made a vital contribution to the history of science, for it led directly to the serious study of astronomy. A number of Renaissance astrologers—Tycho Brahe, Nicolaus Copernicus, Johannes Kepler—became pioneering astronomers; their desire to penetrate the gauze of the heavens helped advance our knowledge of outer space in revolutionary ways. Weather too was long thought to be dictated by stars, meteors and planets, and when today's forecasters are feeling their oats, they like to be called meteorologists.

Because astrology has played so significant a role in human history, its influence is everywhere in society, language and arts, perhaps second only to that of religion. A study of astrology takes us on a whirlwind tour through human culture: Mesopotamiian stargazers gave us the zodiac (and the three Magi, astrologer-priests who witnessed Christ's birth); Egyptians created the idea of the horoscope; the Greeks gave us the constellations, the organizing units of European astrology, and their fanciful, evocative names.

However much astrology has enriched our history, poetry and language, it is, in scientific terms, utter bunk. In a shattering 1995 attack on astrology printed in Britain's *Independent* newspaper, Richard Dawkins, the British scientist and writer who is an especially avid foe of pseudoscience, recalled an anecdote about film director Otto Preminger. An enthusiast of astrology once approached the director on a movie set and inquired, "Gee, Mr. Preminger, what sign are you?" The famed grouch flashed an icy glare and replied, "I am a do-not-disturb sign."

**as science has replaced superstition in men's affairs, astrology's influence has, so to speak, entered retrograde**

STAR POWER Worlds of wonder in the heavens, the constellations named by the Greeks continue to inform modern astrology. Above, the constellations of the southern hemisphere are on the left, the northern hemisphere on the right in these maps painted by Briton James Thornhill in 1725. The main picture of a distant star cluster was taken by the Hubble Space Telescope

# where geometry is fate

The Bermuda Triangle has been three sides of trouble from the get-go. The first written record we have of human beings entering this region of the Atlantic Ocean bounded roughly by modern-day Miami, Puerto Rico and Bermuda speaks of mysterious doings. In 1492, days before he landed in the New World, Christopher Columbus recorded in his log that as the *Santa María* passed through, its compass began gyrating wildly, a strange light appeared on the horizon and a bolt of fire fell from the sky. In the centuries since, sailors have recounted more tales of unexplainable, sinister happenings in the area. But mariners like to spin yarns, and their superstitions about the area seemed similar to many other sea fables—until Dec. 5, 1945.

On that day, Flight 19—a group of five Navy Avenger fighter-bombers—took off from the Fort Lauderdale Naval Air Station. During the routine three-hour training mission, the 14 aviators involved were to practice bombing and low-level strafing off the Florida coast. A few hours later, the mission commander, Lieut. Charles Taylor, radioed back that his compasses weren't working and

he was lost. After several additional, increasingly garbled distress calls, nothing more was heard. Hours later, a Martin Mariner with 13 crewmen aboard, one of hundreds of aircraft launched to search for Flight 19, also vanished. No wreckage and no bodies were ever found.

The mystery impressed a young officer who investigated it, Charles Berlitz. He researched similar incidents for decades, joined by E.V.W. Jones, an Associated Press reporter. In 1950, on a slow news day in September, Jones persuaded his editor to put a story on the wires detailing the mysteries surrounding this part of the ocean. It was the first time that a paranormal explanation was advanced for what had, until then, seemed like a series of tragic accidents.

It was far from the last. In 1964, writer Vincent Gaddis coined the term "Bermuda Triangle" for an article in *Argosy* magazine. Ten years later, Berlitz pulled together all the research he had done since 1945 for a book with the same name; it became a huge best seller.

In the years since, explanations for the disappearances floated before a transfixed public have ranged from the standard (UFO

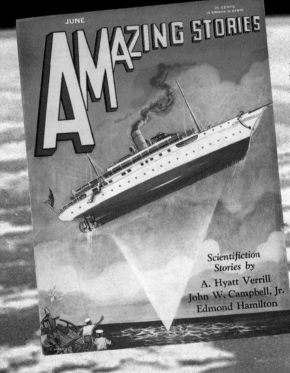

**HYPOTENUSE OF HORROR!** The Bermuda Triangle may not be able to levitate ocean liners, as this 1930 sci-fi magazine suggested, but these 500,000 sq. mi. of the Atlantic invite both serious scientific scrutiny and the wackiest of paranormal hypotheses. Tidal waves, alien abduction, a gill-breathing race of undersea beings—all have been proposed as agents in the documented disappearances here

abductions) to the absurd (our favorite: power generators still functioning in the sunken city of Atlantis are discharging energy rays). The idea that strange forces lurk in the Atlantic has never quite left the radar screen of our collective imaginations. Believers note that both the U.S. Navy and Coast Guard say the area is one of a handful of places in the world where compasses point to true, rather than magnetic, north—an anomaly that could lead to deadly confusion for ships and planes. Doubters, who prefer actuaries to anecdotes, note that the cold-eyed insurers at Lloyd's of London declared in the late 1990s, "The Bermuda Triangle does not exist … there are just as many losses as in other wide expanses of ocean."

One recent, compelling theory about the Triangle relates to little-understood gas compounds known as clathrates. Similar in appearance and chemical structure to ice, these large solids form when gas is released underwater at just the right temperature and pressure. In recent years, vast fields of methane clathrates have been discovered deep in the waters roughly corresponding to the Bermuda Triangle.

Although clathrates are usually stable, rising temperatures can cause them to dissolve, releasing the gas trapped inside, which then rises to the water's surface. Geochemist Richard McIver theorizes that when clathrate deposits on the ocean floor beneath the Triangle dissolve, the water above fizzes like champagne as the gas is released. Ships passing overhead at that moment could sink, because the water supporting them becomes temporarily less dense. Even airplanes could be affected, as large rising bubbles of gas create turbulence, perhaps asphyxiating pilots—or bursting into flames on contact with hot engines.

The Triangle continues to breed questions. One mystery seemed to have been dispelled in May 1991, when the wreckage of five Navy Avengers was found in 600 ft. of water, about 10 miles from Fort Lauderdale. But the mystery only deepened a few days later, when a check of identification numbers showed that these were not the planes of the missing Flight 19—even though the Navy had no record of another group of five Avengers being lost in that area.

■ the area is one of a handful of places in the world where compasses point to true, rather than magnetic, north— an anomaly that could lead to deadly confusion

**FLIGHT 19** This picture shows both the ground crew supporting the pilot training mission as well as the 14 men who went missing on Dec. 5, 1945. Three years later, on Jan. 31, 1948, the airliner *Star Tiger* vanished while flying over the area with 29 people aboard

**MISSING** The U.S.S. *Cyclops* vanished in the Triangle in May 1918, with 306 men aboard. It is one of many reports of ships sinking or vanishing in the region—although skeptics say many of the tales are exaggerated or can be easily explained by natural forces

# the dinosaurs' downfall? it came from outer space

How and why did the dinosaurs pass from Earth? Since British scientist Richard Owen coined the term—which means "terrible lizard"—in 1842, scientists have struggled to explain the sudden demise of the creatures. For some 160 million years, they were the dominant life-form on the planet, the apex of the animal kingdom. Yet their story, preserved in an extensive fossil record, comes to an abrupt end around 65 million years ago. Their extinction, generations of scientists suspected, must have been due to some sort of cataclysmic natural disaster: a plague or worldwide drought, perhaps a drastic shift in Earth's climate or atmosphere.

The answer to the mysterious demise of the dinosaurs emerged from one of the great unexplained events of the 20th century. On June 30, 1908, something exploded near the Tunguska River in Siberia. Trees in a nine-mile radius from ground zero were incinerated; those in a 25-mile radius were felled—some 60 million of them. The blast occurred in such a remote region of Russia that it was not until 1927 that scientists mounted an expedition to explore it. They found that the ground near the blast crater contained high levels of iridium, a substance very rare on Earth but prevalent on asteroids. The eventual conclusion: the Tunguska Event was caused when a meteorite at

BIG BANG Above, this skull and neck of a velociraptor were found in Mongolia. Right, an artist depicts a meteor striking the planet, The crater in the photocomposite at left is Meteor Crater in Arizona; it is 4,000 ft. in diameter and 570 ft. deep. In short: ouch!

## the answer to the creatures' mysterious demise emerged from one of the great unexplained events of the 20th century

least 100 ft. in diameter exploded five miles above the ground.

In 1980 physicist Luis Alvarez and his son Walter advanced a startling theory: perhaps a meteor impact similar to that at Tunguska had ended the age of the dinosaurs. The primary evidence: in soil core samples taken in locations all around the globe, iridium had been found in a thin layer of clay that formed the boundary between the fossil-rich rock of the Cretaceous period, the end of the dinosaur age, and the sparsely fossiled rock of the Tertiary period that followed. Alvarez's hypothesis: a monster extraterrestrial body had slammed into the planet, sending an enormous fireball into the

stratosphere, along with vast amounts of debris. A great cloud of dust enshrouded Earth, blocking sunlight for months, even years. In the ensuing cold and dark, plants and animals perished. When the dust shroud eventually settled back to Earth, it formed the telltale worldwide layer of iridium in the clay. Some scientists scoffed. Then, in 1990, scientists realized a crater some 112 miles in diameter below the town of Chicxulub on the northern tip of Mexico's Yucatán Peninsula, found in 1978, might be the culprit. The crater was dated at 65 million years old, strong evidence that the dinosaurs' demise was caused by forces that came from beyond this world.

SANFORD—AGLIOLO—CORBIS

43

# wizards of water

Water means life in agrarian societies, and few needs are more compelling than locating it. For centuries, adepts of the practice called dowsing have led the search, oftentimes holding a rudimentary tool, a Y-shaped stick with a projecting end. The dowser walks across a landscape, waiting for the stick to move seemingly of its own volition, swerving down toward the ground. When it does—eureka!—the dowser has divined his precious hidden quarry.

Dowsing goes by many names—divining, water witching, radiesthesia—and it employs a variety of tools in addition to the classic forked stick: a pair of L-shaped brass rods is the choice of many dowsers, while radiesthesia refers to the practice of dangling an object over a map and noting its movements to reveal hidden targets. Thanks to the apparent success of many venerable dowsers, their methods are used to search for treasures in addition to water: gems and minerals, gold and oil.

Because dowsers often find water, their art is one of the most widely accepted forms of unexplained phenomena. The mystery of dowsing boils down to a single question: How does the dowser receive his information? Many practitioners are convinced that a good dowser has the power to sense forces that others cannot. They argue that mankind will eventually come to understand these forces, whether they are magnetic, radioactive, electrical or perhaps not yet known to science. For their part, scientists—who realized long ago that seemingly quaint folk practices can be doorways to discovery—have created blind tests that subject dowsing to rigorous scrutiny.

Sadly for believers, these tests have failed to establish that dowsing really works, much less that it holds clues to hidden forces. In test after test, dowsers of good reputation failed to find their quarry more often than random participants did. Scientists draw a number of conclusions from these tests: they suspect that master dowsers rely on an acquired knowledge of geography and topography to help them find their targets. They ascribe the sudden downturn of the divining rod to the ideomotor effect, an involuntary body movement evoked by a thought process rather than by outside simulation. In short, they argue, the dowser reacts to internal cues rather than external forces.

Yet the art of dowsing remains one of the more puzzling of mysterious phenomena, simply because it so often seems to work in the field, if not under scientific conditions. Confusion prevails: the U.S. Geological Survey declared in 1977 that dowsing was a pseudo-science, yet the Army Corps of Engineers has employed dowsers. And one can join reputable dowsing societies in nations around the world. Perhaps that is what makes the failure to explain dowsing through science so frustrating. Its proponents are not the kooks or cranks familiar to those exploring unexplained phenomena: they are more often down-to-earth folks, who say dowsing works for them and that science will catch up some day. Even James Randi, the former magician who is a professional skeptic of parapsychology, has good words for them. On his website, *www.randi.org,* the oft-scornful Randi compares them to other advocates of the paranormal and declares, "No claimants even approach the dowsers for honesty. These are persons who are genuinely, thoroughly, self-deceived." Or maybe just ahead of their time?

**HOT ROD** This dowser uses the classic Y-shaped stick as a divining rod. The tool was first described by German scholar and metallurgist Georgius Agricola in 1556

BETTMANN/CORBIS

## scientists realized long ago that seemingly quaint folk practices are often doorways to discovery

# we all shine on

Semyon Davidovich Kirlian, a Soviet electrician, was repairing some hospital equipment in his workshop near the Black Sea in 1939 when a spark jumped from his hand to a metal probe. Curious, he repeated the procedure, this time with his hand pressed against a photographic plate, and then developed the film. What Kirlian saw amazed him—a ghostly image of his palm and fingers, surrounded by a faint, halolike "aura."

Kirlian had only the vaguest understanding of what he was looking at. A trained scientist might have begun a rigorous investigation of this phenomenon, but the electrician had no background as a researcher, and his mind gravitated toward the metaphysical possibilities of his discovery. Soon he declared that he had found a process for imaging the supernatural energy that animates all living things. In effect, he claimed, he had invented a way to take pictures of the soul.

In truth, the human body radiates all sorts of energy at low levels. The nervous system generates electromagnetism. Mechanical processes, such as breathing and the beating of one's heart, emit sonic vibrations. And since every one of our cells is a miniscule energy plant, our bodies also radiate heat. Each of these emanations can be measured (by galvanometers, sonograms and infrared cameras, respectively) and used to create a spectral-looking image of the body. But none of the resulting visions are even remotely mystical.

Kirlian believed his process captured something else, something metaphysical. When he photographed a leaf with electric current passing through it, its "life force" appeared in outline, just as with images of his hand. When he cut away a section of the leaf and photographed it again, part of the leaf was missing (as would be expected), but its aura inexplicably retained the shape and profile of the original. Now this was very interesting indeed—except subsequent researchers have been able to duplicate that result only when using the same photographic plate twice, which leads them to assume that the recurring image is the result of the residue of the first image on the plate, rather than invisible biological energy.

After much investigation, several teams of scientists decided that Kirlian had stumbled upon a novel way to create images of electrical discharge, in much the same way that Van de Graaff generators create beautiful patterns of light when

**HAZED AND CONFUSED Semyon D. Kirlian believed his images showed the soul, but these recent Kirlian photos show that even coins will emanate a shimmering aura if charged with electricity**

they give off sparks of static electricity. But that was the end of the mystery. They refuted Kirlian's claims about picturing the life force by demonstrating that almost any object, whether living or inanimate, could be made to glow in Kirlian photos simply by passing an electric current through it.

Kirlian's photographs captured imaginations, if not souls. The powerful idea that each of us projects emanations of various kinds has become a central tenet of a wide variety of New Age beliefs and therapies, many of them of questionable merit, if harmless. To a certain extent, the notion of the aura has replaced the notion of the soul in many New Age views of life; both are stand-ins for the ineffable spirit that resides within us. Whether that spirit is available for Kodak moments remains to be seen.

By the late 1960s and '70s, researchers had concluded that Kirlian's discovery had no scientific merit. That judgment, however, turned out to be premature. In the 1980s, engineers realized that the imaging technique Kirlian had invented could be used to detect internal flaws within the structural components of airplanes and spacecraft, as well as weaknesses within precision-tooled metal parts, like turbine blades—all without cutting them open and thus rendering them useless. Which means that even if Kirlian didn't find a way to photograph souls, he did help save lives.

# aligning with the grid

HIGH TIMES Architect C.Y. Lee assumes a lotus position on a rock outside Taiwan's capital, Taipei, over which his 101-story skyscraper looms. A road that dead-ended at the building's side presented a feng shui problem; a fountain was added to redirect the street's energy.

At left are a portable compass and sundial, two traditional tools of the feng shui master, dating from the Ming dynasty (1368-1644). Feng shui was attacked in China during the 1960s: Mao Zedong denounced it as a relic of a burdensome past during the Cultural Revolution, and its masters were persecuted. Only in recent years has it begun to resurface in mainland China.

The tallest building in the world—for the next few years, anyway—is the splendid splinter on the left, the Taipei 101 tower in Taiwan. Its builders brag that the 1,670-ft. structure is the most technologically advanced skyscraper ever built: its offices are wired to the Internet with fiber-optic cables, and its occupants swoosh to work on the world's fastest elevators. On its 88th floor a tuned mass damper—a 730-ton beehive-shaped mass of welded steel plates that moves in opposition to outside forces—helps stabilize the building in the face of high winds and earthquakes. Yet when it came time to design the building's interior, architect C.Y. Lee turned away from technology and handed the job to a practitioner of a 3,500-year-old Asian mystical discipline : a feng shui master.

In recent decades, the once arcane Asian art of feng shui ("wind and water") has become highly popular in the U.S. and other Western nations. At its heart is the attempt to bring man and his works into harmony with nature by channeling the planet's natural flow of electromagnetic energy, which the Chinese call *qi (or Chi)*. The discipline involves manipulating the shape, size and color of a structure as well as its entrances. A building that allows *qi* to flow freely is said to have good feng shui, which brings prosperity and success. In ancient China, the art was used to orient streets, buildings and neighborhoods, even entire villages and cities.

The sense that the planet's surface is a network of lines or zones of powerful force is not unique to Asia; in Britain and elsewhere in Europe, the search for "ley lines," sometimes called earth-dragon lines, was begun by the publication of amateur archaeologist Alfred Watkins' book *The Old Straight Track* in 1921. Readers of *The Da Vinci Code* will recall the "rose lines" that are one key to the characters' search for the Holy Grail. In Australia Aboriginal peoples practice "walkabouts," spiritual pilgrimages taken along invisible tracks the late travel writer Bruce Chatwin called "songlines." There is science as well as mystery in such supposed lines of force: human life is sustained by the planet's magnetic field, as revealed in the polar auroras, where errant particles of the sun's dangerous cosmic wind that are not deflected by Earth's atmosphere shimmer and glow.

Some scholars argue that feng shui's origins can be traced further back than 3,500 B.C., to astrological maps created around 6,000 B.C. Chinese astrology indeed played a key role in classic feng shui. But as the practice has developed in the West, it has acquired a New Age patina that is deeply troubling to its more orthodox proponents: a quick Google search will take you to the serious folks at the American Feng Shui Institute, who promise to "correct mistakes ... discern imposters ... and set feng shui apart from superstition, mysticism and religion." Or you can visit a site that promises, more succinctly, to help feng shui "shed its snake-oil-and-incense message."

If you're one of those who think feng shui is way too twee, help may be at hand: a January 2005 story in TIME's Asia edition featured the latest craze in Asian arts, a 16th century Japanese discipline known as *wabi-sabi*. Super-duper!

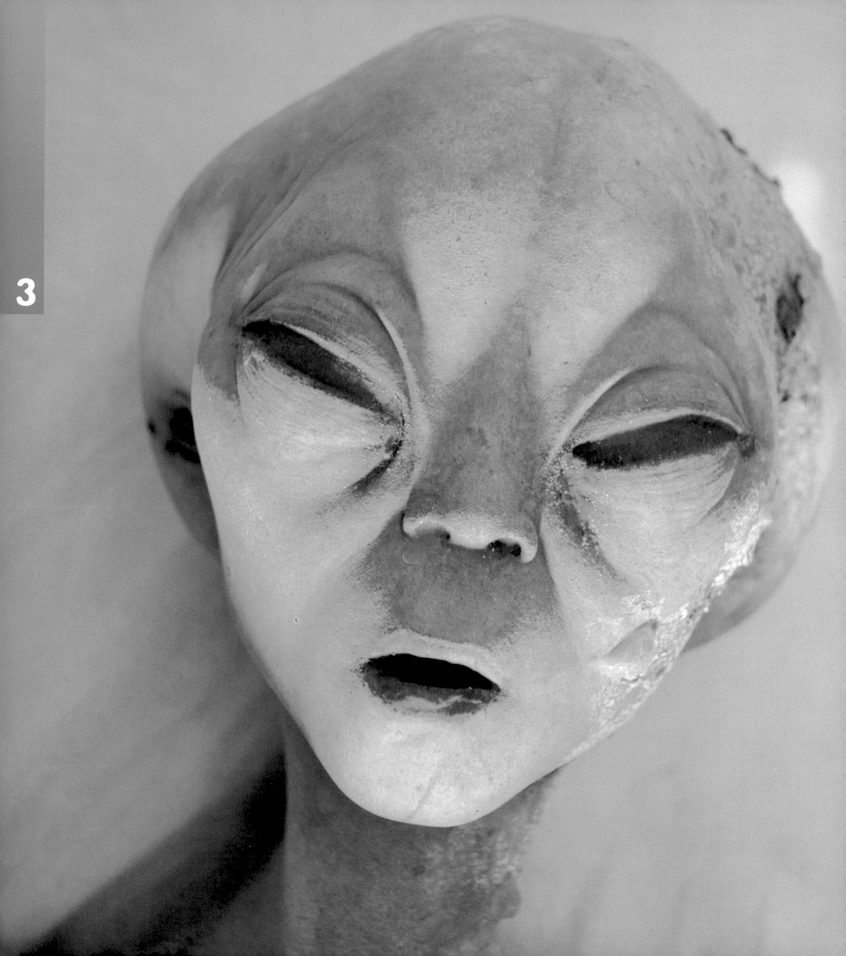

# Mysteries of Space

"I believe that the extraordinary should be pursued. But extraordinary claims require extraordinary evidence" —Carl Sagan

# Under Roswell's Spell

**Roswell Daily Record**

RECORD PHONES
Business Office 2288
News Department 2287

Movies as Usual

GRAND

Claims Army
Is Stacking
Courts Martial

Indiana Senator
Lays Protest
Before Patterson

**RAAF Captures Flying Saucer
On Ranch in Roswell Region**

House Passes
Tax Slash by
Large Margin

Defeat Amendment
By Demos to Remove
Many from Rolls

Security Council
Paves Way to Talks
On Arms Reductions

No Details of
Flying Disk
Are Revealed

Roswell Hardware
Man and Wife
Report Disk Seen

Ex-King Carol Weds Mme. Lupescu

Born amid confusion, nurtured by rumor and complicated by official deceit, the incidents that took place in Roswell, N.M., in the summer of 1947 have become a modern myth of baroque proportions. Almost six decades after they occurred, the facts in the case amount to a few shiny needles of truth adrift in a haystack of hypotheticals. So let's boil down the Roswell story to its three major parts: 1. Wreckage of unknown origin was found near this small New Mexico town. 2. Witnesses later reported seeing a crashed spaceship and tiny alien bodies. 3. Some of the facts were hushed up by a long-running government cover-up.

The only thing we know for certain is that the last of those three statements is true. So let's consider them one at a time.

The story begins with rancher W.W. (Mac) Brazel. On June 14, 1947, he was making his rounds at the J.B. Foster sheep ranch, 85 miles northwest of Roswell, when he chanced upon strange debris—rubber strips, tinfoil, wood sticks, Scotch tape and other tape with a floral design—strewn over a 200-yd. swath of desert. The origin of the mess was unclear.

Ten days after Brazel's discovery, pilot Kenneth Arnold was flying near Washington State's Cascade Mountains when he spotted what he described as nine disklike objects flying in formation at about 1,200 m.p.h. Arnold's report, which remains unexplained, spawned copycat tales, and by July 4, hundreds of sightings of "flying saucers" across the nation had been reported.

But Brazel was unaware of these sightings until July 5, when he drove to the nearby town of Corona, heard about the saucers and may have learned of a rumored reward for anyone who recovered one. By then, Brazel had gathered the debris and taken it home. On July 7 he told Sheriff George Wilcox that he might have found a flying disk; the sheriff soon collected the debris, then phoned nearby Roswell Army Air Field (RAAF), home of the 509th Bomb Group, and notified an intelligence officer of the discovery.

The group's commander, Colonel William Blanchard, told press officer Walter Haut, "We have in our possession a flying saucer. This thing crashed north of Roswell, and we've shipped it all to General Ramey, 8th Air Force at Fort Worth." Haut issued a press release, and the next morning the Roswell *Daily Record* carried the headline at left: RAAF CAPTURES FLYING SAUCER ON RANCH IN ROSWELL REGION.

The furor was short-lived. At 8th Air Force headquarters, Brigadier General Roger Ramey called in the local press and announced that the debris was the remnants not of a saucer but of a high-altitude weather balloon. The sticks and tinfoil, he explained, were from a reflector used to track the balloon by radar. Tranquillity returned to New Mexico.

Three decades would pass before interest in the story was rekindled by the 1980 book *The Roswell Incident*. Mentioned briefly in the book was a secondhand yarn involving New Mexican Grady (Barney) Barnett, who claimed to have come upon a crashed saucer on the Plains of San Agustin, N.M., about 150 miles west of the Foster ranch, in 1947. Before being shooed away by military police, he claimed, he had spotted several little bodies strewn nearby.

This tale had legs: the authors of the 1991 book *UFO Crash at Roswell* charged that the government had spirited away the remains of the ship's crew, several little alien bodies. After the book's publication, several other witnesses came forward to offer further elaborations on this story, giving it additional credence.

Roswell-mania! The U.S. government was by now under so much fire for its alleged cover-ups of the various incidents that the Air Force held inquiries into the case, interviewing as many witnesses as possible. In 1994 an Air Force report admitted for the first time that there had been a cover-up. Brazel's find, it said, was not wreckage from a weather balloon; instead, it was from a balloon train carrying acoustical equipment designed to monitor Soviet nuclear tests under top-secret Project Mogul. One such probe was launched on June 4 and was tracked to within 20 miles of the Foster ranch before it disappeared from the radar in mid-June.

That account seemed to resolve the first element of the Roswell legend, but it did not address the second, charges that alien bodies had been found. That subject was addressed in a 1997 report, which declared that in the 1950s the Air Force conducted experiments in which small dummies were dropped into the desert from high-altitude balloons to study the results of the impact. Witnesses' descriptions of the Roswell "aliens" closely match the characteristics of the dummies: 4 ft. tall, bluish skin color and no ears, hair, eyebrows or eyelashes.

The glaring problem with this story: the crash tests took place in the mid-1950s. The report suggested that time and faulty memories had falsely conflated the events, so those who saw the dummies in the 1950s later believed they had seen them in 1947 instead.

Sound fishy? Yes—and once the government admitted some of its original 1947 story had been a fiction, it opened itself to the charge that everything it has ever said about Roswell has been an elaborate, decades-long cover-up.

And guess what, dear reader? If you choose to believe that something involving aliens happened in New Mexico in 1947, Washington's official version of America's most famous UFO case isn't going to convince you otherwise. The only thing we know for sure is this: the truth is out there. In this case, swaddled in six decades of legend, lore and lies, it's way out there.

# Manna from Heaven

In a world that contains inexplicable wonders, some things are all too explicable. When it's springtime at Loch Ness, sightings of "Nessie" are apt to heat up, just as the first tourists arrive. And when the merchants of Roswell, N.M., realized that they could turn little green men into long green currency, they converted their town into America's foremost alien-themed tourist trap

**CASHING IN:** A Roswell exhibit re-creates the supposed scene of the 1947 alien landings. As Bill Pope of the Roswell Chamber of Commerce explained to TIME in 1997, "I've been in a lot of communities in my lifetime. I was near a community in Oklahoma that had the champion cow-chip-throwing contest. And there's a little community not far from us over here that has lizard races ... We have something to create interest and an inflow of people, and that creates dollars and that's what we're all about."

**FRENZY:** If an alien space-ship really did crash-land in New Mexico, the event would be among the most momentous in human history. Yet if "the truth is out there," it has been well obscured by almost six decades of fantasy, fable and folly.

**WHEE!** Those who express sincere interest in UFOs often struggle to be taken seriously—and no wonder. Legitimate scientific inquiry into the possibility of alien visitations to Earth has been hijacked by kooks, cranks, profiteers and Hollywood screenwriters who continue to trivialize the subject. The appetite for UFOs seems inexhaustible. America's fascination with them, which surged in the late 1940s, has never tapered off. Five decades after the 1947 incident in Roswell, a TIME poll showed that 65% of Americans believed a UFO had crash-landed there.

So why spoil the fun? Here are some post-cards from Roswell, many of them dating from the small town's big 1997 party celebrating the 50th anniversary of the legendary sightings.

# Intelligent Designs?

**SICILY** Two objects appear to be plainly visible in the sky in this famous photo, taken in Taormina on Dec. 10, 1954. A UFO study group in Italy recently claimed to have exposed the photograph as a hoax: the photo, they said, is a double exposure, in which the two objects were added to the original image. Note that the men are actually looking a bit to the right of the two apparent UFOs. The late 1940s and early 1950s saw a rash of reports of UFOs, not only in the U.S., but also in Europe.

Perhaps the single greatest unexplained mystery of the past six decades is the worldwide upsurge in reports of strange objects that fly through the skies at high speed, often in formation and often exhibiting behavior that suggests they are the product of intelligent design far in advance of mankind's current technology. Depending on one's point of view, the rash of unexplained sightings can be seen as authentic natural mysteries, as fascinating examples of mass delusion and modern mythmaking or as evidence of conspiracies by world governments to suppress proof of alien visitations to Earth. If you are one of those who believe that in this universe we are not alone—well, you *are* not alone: in 1997 some 80% of Americans told TIME they believed that the U.S. government knows more than it is saying about the craft dubbed unidentified flying objects, or UFOs.

Science-fiction writers of the late 19th and early 20th centuries explored the notion of alien cultures; examples include H.G. Wells' *War of the Worlds,* the Buck Rogers comic strips and films and E.R. Burroughs' John Carter of Mars series. Yet we can identify the exact starting point of the world's current fascination with UFOs. In fact, we can read about it in the July 14, 1947, issue of TIME, which declared,

*The first man to report seeing them was Kenneth Arnold, of Boise, Idaho. Arnold, a businessman, was flying near Washington's Mt. Rainier when nine saucerlike objects, noiseless and sunbright, came streaking over the Cascades at "1,200 miles an hour in formation, like the tail of a kite," Arnold said later. "I don't believe it, but I saw it." Newspapers spread the story. Scientists put it down to spots before the eyes. Then other reports began to come in. Stovepipes. Washtubs. In Seattle, 15 persons in one day called the papers to report having seen "flying saucers." Two Portland deputy sheriffs spotted "20 in a line going like hell to the west."*

TIME's story went on to recount the testimony of veteran airline pilot E.J. Smith, who reported seeing four or five "somethings" that flew in formation with his United Air Lines plane for 45 miles, until they vanished in a burst of speed. Note the date of these events: yes, that was the same summer as the famous Roswell, N.M., incidents.

What's fascinating about these early events is that they encapsulate almost all the subsequent furor over UFOs: the observation by witnesses generally considered reliable, like pilot Smith; the attempts by scientists to explain the sightings as natural (spots before the eyes); the suspicion, generated at Roswell, that the government is covering up the truth about the sightings.

Almost 60 years later, little has changed. Today the community of UFO believers includes brilliant, inquiring individuals—and utter wackos. Eyewitnesses with little to gain continue to report seeing strange craft in the sky, for which science can offer no explanation. Hoaxers go on taking pictures of Frisbees and passing them off as UFOs, just for laughs. And only 20% of Americans expect their government to tell them the truth about UFOs.

Many UFO sightings are caused by natural phenomena, but some remain utterly inexplicable. And then there are those that have been called hoaxes—among them, the three UFO pictures shown here.

MASSACHUSETTS The U.S. Air Force conducted evaluations of UFOs from 1948 through 1969; from 1952 on, the study was named Project Blue Book. One well-known photograph reviewed by the group was this image of four bright lights taken by U.S. Coast Guard photographer Shell Alpert in Salem, Mass., in 1952, a year of many sightings. The analysts declared the photo was a fake; 11 years later they reopened the case, discounted the hoax theory and concluded that the lights were interior reflections on the window glass. Critics charge that Project Blue Book was a way for the U.S. government to appear to take UFO reports seriously, while the team's leaders were determined to find no evidence of UFOs.

OHIO Zanesville barber Ralph Ditter took this well-known photo on Nov. 13, 1966. He claimed the craft he saw was about 30 ft. long and was a good distance from his camera. The image was studied by photo experts at the Rand Corporation, who concluded the picture was faked: they believed the object shown was 3 to 4 in. in diameter and only 3 to 4 ft. from the camera. Ditter later confessed the photo was taken as a joke; he had used a hubcap from his daughters' wagon as the alien craft. For better or for worse, hoaxes like this one, weird suicidal cults and the nonsensical claims about alien life made by some UFO enthusiasts have long convinced most serious scientists that stories of UFO sightings do not merit investigation.

# Cereal Thrillers

"We wanted people to think that a UFO had landed in a field, when it was really just two blokes with a plank of wood," artist Doug Bowers told a reporter from Britain's *Sunday Telegraph* in 2002, a year when worldwide interest in crop circles spiked, thanks to the success of M. Night Shyamalan's spooky film *Signs*. Bowers' cohort in the cornfield was fellow artist Dave Chorley; their pioneering creations, crop circles that began appearing in Wiltshire in the late 1970s, caused a sensation. Strange signs began, well, cropping up around the world, as fellow "cerealogists" and "croppies" learned that with a few simple tools—boards, rope, beer—a couple of blokes could create a mystifying set of "alien" symbols in a farmer's field in only an hour or so.

Bowers and Chorley finally fessed up to their hoax in 1991. Bowers admitted that "we used to mingle with [crowds of sightseers] and listen to what they were saying, all these so-called UFO experts spouting off about aliens. We would look at each and burst out laughing." For anyone who doubts that there is fellowship in the rings, log on to *circlemakers.org* and share the joy of Britain's master grain glyphers.

And yet ... those who believe unknown forces are at work here may just be right, especially if we define those forces as aspects of natural science we do not yet understand. Yes, scientists believe at least 80% of the circles are "pranks with planks"—but what about the rest? Reputable investigators have found phenomena not made by man in some crop circles, including grain stems that are uniformly bent into angles rather than broken; expulsion cavities (holes blown out at nodes) in plants; an increase in crystallinity in subsoil minerals, a result of high pressure and temperature. Moreover, many "real" crop circles occur over terrain rich in limestone, which can collect water carrying an electrical charge. One hypothesis: some crop circles are created by microwave energy bursts released by charged plasma. These phenomena might be similar to ball-lightning events, which were long mistakenly labeled "ghost lights." Most folks don't believe in ghosts anymore, but aliens are very much in vogue.

**CROPARAZZI?** These sets of crop circles are very likely the work of hoaxers. Left, California; right, southern England

"When a myth is shared by a large number of people, it becomes a reality" —Motto of Britain's Circlemakers

# Too-Close Encounters

**TAKEN?** The Hills, right, were the first to report that they had been abducted by aliens. Barney Hill died in 1969, eight years after the alleged event; Betty Hill died in 2004. Some students of the Hill case note that the pair may have felt the psychological burden of being an interracial couple in 1960s America, when such marriages were rare. Betty Hill always denied that this was the case

Skeptics often claim that stories of unidentified flying objects and alien abductions are examples of "shared cultural delusions"—not unlike the frenzy that overcame Puritan settlers in 17th century Massachusetts, as hysterical witch hunts spawned the execution of innocent people. Yet we can actually point to the date and time when the very first story of alien abduction was told. The tellers were a married couple, Betty and Barney Hill. And they recounted a tale that has become eerily familiar: the New Hampshire residents claimed they were kidnapped from their bed on Sept. 16, 1961, and taken aboard an alien spacecraft, where big-headed, wide-eyed beings took a sample of Barney's sperm and stuck a needle in Betty's belly button.

The Hills' told their tale in John G. Fuller's 1966 bestseller *The Interrupted Journey*. Their conviction was striking enough to make a believer of John Mack, the late Harvard University psychiatrist and paranormal enthusiast. The story resonated with Americans: in the years after it became public, hundreds, then thousands of fellow abductees began coming forward to recount their stories, which often featured strikingly similar scenarios: nighttime transport to an alien spacecraft; an encounter with beings with bald heads, small noses and oversized, bulging eyes; a humiliating probe of body cavities by alien instruments; a return to the victims' homes followed by a period of amnesia; eventual recovery of the memories through the intercession of a psychiatrist or hypnotist.

Recovered memory—yes, there's the rub. Doubters of such tales point out that no one has ever returned with hard proof of a close encounter with an alien. As skeptical astronomer Carl Sagan dared to point out about the hundreds of reported abductions: "It's surprising more of the neighbors haven't noticed." Betty Hill, for instance, first recalled snatches of her abduction during a series of nightmares that

she told Barney about; the pair recovered their memories later, under hypnosis. Mack, who interviewed and analyzed hundreds of alleged abductees, relied almost exclusively on recovered-memory techniques to elicit the stories he offered as proof of such encounters.

Doubters of abduction stories do not question the sincerity of those who advance them, but some researchers are increasingly convinced that many of the cases can be explained by the brain state that psychologists call "sleep paralysis." This condition, known as the hypnagogic state, occurs sometimes just before we fall off to sleep. Although it only lasts for a few seconds at most, by a trick of perception it can sometimes feel as if it has lasted for hours. Tales of the abduction experience—the feeling that one is unable to move or speak, the sense that some sort of "other" is present, a wash of overwhelming fear and humiliation, the inability to move or even cry out—are parallel in every detail to the symptoms of sleep paralysis.

When a case of sleep paralysis is heightened by a vivid memory or a cultural reference that lingers in the subconscious, the result can make for a convincing but utterly false memory. Perhaps just such a combination was at work on Betty Hill. She may have watched an episode of the classic 1960s science-fiction TV series *The Outer Limits* that featured a wide-eyed alien. The show was broadcast well after the alleged incident—but only 12 days before she first relived her abduction experience under hypnosis. And of course, victims of sleep paralysis with an interest in UFOs can now draw upon a vast trove of abduction accounts in order to furnish the *mise-en-scène* for their own close encounters.

Could most of the stories of alien abduction be little more than psychological delusions? If the skeptics are right, the unknown realms glimpsed in mass stories of alien kidnappings may be not the outer limits of space but the uncharted regions of the human mind.

# Celestial Messages

Sightings of UFOs are among the most prominent evidence for alleged alien visitations to Earth; among others are the weird cases of cattle mutilations reported around the U.S. Some believers find alien influences in ancient creations: Egypt's pyramids or Peru's Nazca lines. Scientists are now pursuing the search for extraterrestrial intelligence (SETI) from Earth—and in space

**HERE'S THE DISH:** The enormous radiotelescope at Arecibo, Puerto Rico, was completed in 1963; it is 1,000 ft. in diameter and covers 20 acres. The big bowl both receives and broadcasts information, bouncing radio signals off distant objects to reveal their composition. In 1974 it beamed the Arecibo Interstellar Message toward M13, a globular star cluster 25,000 light-years away; the signal contained 1,679 bits of data on everything from Earth's position in the solar system to the chemical makeup of the atmosphere. Arecibo scanned the heavens for alien radio transmissions during 1992, but the U.S. Congress halted funding for the program; it continues under private sponsorship.

**GOLDEN OLDIES:** Astronomer Carl Sagan, an early proponent of SETI, was one of those who lobbied NASA to include messages from Earth on missions heading for deep space. The first result: a plaque made of gold-anodized aluminum was attached to the 1972 Pioneer 10 probe. The 9-in. by 6-in. plaque, bottom, shows a man and woman, the spacecraft's outline, the element hydrogen—and more. For two 1977 Voyager probes, NASA created a "golden record," which includes natural sounds, messages in 55 languages and the music of Bach, Beethoven and—roll over, Beethoven!—Chuck Berry. Thirty years later, LPs are obsolete on Earth, if not in other galaxies.

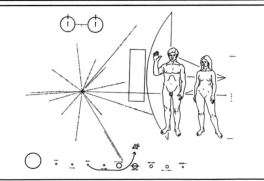

**RUNWAY?** Is this a landing strip for spaceships? Located high in the plains of Peru, this Nazca line certainly looks as if it could be—and that was enough for Swiss author Erich von Däniken, whose influential 1970 book, *Chariots of the Gods,* offered the compelling theory that alien astronauts had visited Earth long ago. Von Däniken's musings tied together many ancient puzzles: the chariot seen by the prophet Ezekiel was a spaceship; the Nazca lines were created for alien craft; the heads on Easter Island are aliens' work. The public loved the theories; scientists almost universally dismissed them at the time—and still do.

**CATTLE MUTILATIONS:** One of the first widely reported cases of a weird livestock death was in Alamosa, Colo., in 1967. Since then hundreds of cows and horses are said to have been killed and mutilated by unknown agencies. Some blame natural predators; farmers disagree. Worth noting: many reports come from down-to-earth folk rather than UFO enthusiasts.

# Dreamland in the Desert

Looking for aliens? Take a drive across sunny Nevada along the Extraterrestrial Highway. About 100 miles north of Las Vegas, smack dab in the remotest reaches of the desert, stop for a burger at the Little A'le'Inn diner in the tiny town of Rachel, and you'll be close to a vast, secret U.S. Air Force installation that takes up some 8,000 sq. mi. This outpost in the desert is often referred to as Area 51, though the base is so secret it has no official name.

Enjoy the view of the desert, because you aren't going to get any closer to Area 51, much less inside, and here's why: this is the one place on Earth where human beings routinely interact with alien life. Both the wreckage of crashed alien spaceships and the bodies of dead aliens have been brought here, where NASA scientists toil in a vast underground facility, attempting to reverse-engineer the technology behind the extraterrestrial craft. The so-called Cheshire Airstrip, perhaps used as a landing strip for alien spaceships, is also here, though it only appears when water has been sprayed onto its surface of camouflaged asphalt. The land around you is as bleak and desolate as the lunar surface—and that's not a coincidence, for this is where NASA filmed the fake footage of U.S. astronauts supposedly landing on the moon for the six Apollo lunar missions.

Well, that's how the stories go, anyway. In recent years, thanks to *The X-Files*, the 1996 blockbuster movie *Independence Day* and a host of speculative websites, Area 51 has become ground zero for UFO theorists. Writing for TIME in 1997, Walter Kirn called the region a "paranoid Holy Land." The place attracts conspiracy theories like flypaper, even as the U.S. government does its best to keep it a black hole in the desert, from which no information escapes. Those who have tried to penetrate the base's perimeter are monitored by listening devices and cameras posted in the desert, while camo-clad watchers in white jeeps survey them from afar through binoculars. When TIME called the U.S. Air Force to inquire about the place for this book, a spokesman gave us the answer we expected: "We are not going to comment on or discuss this in any way whatsoever."

Something is obviously going on here, so let's examine what we *do* know about this secret desert site. Yes, Area 51 really exists: it is a U.S. Air Force base, the landscape is downright lunar, and Nevada politicians have cashed in on the area's notoriety by naming the nearest interstate the Extraterrestrial Highway. But to date the stories you may have heard about alien life and crashed

spaceships here have never been proved to be more than hypothesis and conjecture. They make wonderful fodder for campfire tales and sci-fi films, but so far they are all fi and no sci.

Yet there's a good reason so many UFO stories revolve around Area 51: it is a testing facility for top-secret, advanced U.S. aircraft. The federally owned land was used for artillery practice during World War II, then by the Atomic Energy Commission for atom bomb tests. In 1955 the Central Intelligence Agency began operating an airfield here, where the first high-altitude spy plane, the U-2, was tested. Soon afterward, defense contractor Lockheed set up a research "skunkworks" at the base, and engineers developed the U-2's successor, the SR-71 Blackbird, here. An estimated 1,000 people lived and worked at the base during the 1960s and '70s. The engineers called the place Dreamland, Paradise Ranch or Groom Lake, after a dry lakebed that runs through the property. In 1977 the first Stealth aircraft, the Lockheed F-117A Nighthawk, was flown here, although the U.S. government did not acknowledge the existence of the plane until 1988.

Reported sightings of UFOs in these parts spiked during the long years of aircraft testing, and no wonder: in addition to Stealth fighters and bombers, the Air Force is believed to have tested vertical take-off and landing aircraft here, as well as one-person flying machines and the drone probes flown during the U.S.-led invasions of Afghanistan and Iraq after 2001. And as for alien craft: the U.S. government did fly and study captured Soviet aircraft here during the cold war, as documents since declassified have shown.

In 2004 a reporter for the St. Petersburg *Times* dropped in on a Florida gathering of former Honeywell engineers who had worked on Lockheed's SR-71 project at Dreamland. At the event, dubbed a "spook reunion," the all-male Area 51 alumni laughed and scoffed at reports that alien craft were ever a part of the Groom Lake story.

Here's another thing we know about Area 51. In 1994, the families of two Defense Department employees who died after working at the base sued the U.S. government, saying the men had been exposed to harmful chemicals during their work at the site; the cases led to reforms on the base. Even so, in 1995 President Bill Clinton signed an Executive Order releasing "the Air Force operating facility near Groom Lake" from federal environmental reporting requirements. George W. Bush has followed suit, renewing the order every year. It's one more way for the government to ensure the truth stays in there.

**WHAT'S OUT THERE?** In the main picture, an unidentified aircraft soars over the Nevada desert above Area 51. The insets show airplane hangars at the secret installation and cameras set up in the remote desert to monitor intruders; the warning sign at right is a bit more old-fashioned. The Air Force is believed to fly a regular daily jet shuttle service to and from Las Vegas to bring its employees to the secret facility. If you don't crave a desert journey, the newest way to see Area 51 is from your desktop—via Google Earth

**WARNING**

**Restricted Area**

It is unlawful to enter this area without permission of the Installation Commander.
Sec. 21, Internal Security Act of 1950; 50 U.S.C.797

While on this Installation all personnel and the property under their control are subject to search.

Use of deadly force authorized.

**WARNING!**
NO TRESPASSING
AUTHORITY N.R.S. 207-200
MAXIMUM PUNISHMENT: $1000 FINE
SIX MONTHS IMPRISONMENT
OR BOTH
STRICTLY ENFORCED

PHOTOGRAPHY
OF THIS AREA
IS PROHIBITED
18 USC 795

# Mars, Mankind's Muse

The great canals that lie along the equatorial region of the planet Mars were first mapped by Italian astronomer Giovanni Schiaparelli, who initially observed the mysterious, long straight lines on the planet's surface through his telescope in 1877. Excited by his discovery, he made lengthy lists of the *canali* (the word means channels; it was mistranslated into English as "canals"). Schiaparelli named hundreds of the long lanes of water, many of them based on classical mythology: Cerberus and Hades, Titan and Hephaestus. The greatest supporter of the Italian's work was the foremost U.S. astronomer of the age, Percival Lowell, who declared that the canals were created by intelligent beings for irrigation. Schiaparelli, obsessed with Mars, also was the first to identify its albedo features, light and dark areas on the planet's surface still visible today.

The bad news: there are no canals on Mars. Schiaparelli, Lowell and many other believers in the canals were utterly off-base about these features, which they glimpsed only as hazy areas of darkness, even when using the best telescopes of the time. The good news: Schiaparelli was right about the Red Planet's albedo features. These markings are locations at which darker-than-normal surface dust is deposited by giant windstorms blowing across the barren, rocky surface of the apparently lifeless, and definitely canal-less, planet.

As Earth's closest planetary neighbor in space, Mars has long been a magnet for musings and a factory for fables. Because of its reddish hue in the sky, the ancients saw it as a world of fire and brimstone: the Babylonians, Greeks and Romans all named it after their god of war (Nergal, Ares and Mars, respectively). The Hebrews gave it a less bellicose name, Ma'adim, "the One Who Blushes."

When the cold war jump-started the age of space exploration, Mars was a natural candidate for investigation, second only to the moon in interest. The first visitor to the planet was a U.S. flyby spacecraft, Mariner 4, launched by NASA in 1964. It passed Mars in July 1965 and sent back the first close-range pictures ever seen of another planet. Since then a flotilla of flyby craft, orbiters and landers have mapped, studied and roamed the planet. We have learned fascinating things about Mars. It may have had much water in the past—and still has some. Like Earth, it has auroras, clouds and polar ice caps (of frozen water and carbon dioxide); dust devils whirl across its surface. However, an unusual number of Mars missions, both Russian and American, have failed in one way or another, leading to notions that a "Bermuda Triangle in space" is hampering exploration.

One might assume that the example of Schiaparelli's canals, coupled with the wealth of information we now have about the Red Planet, would have put an end to wild speculation about Mars. But one would be wrong. Beginning in 1976, a host of far-out theories has sprouted about Mars past and Mars present; they are currently spread by websites that devote page after page of technobabble to

**A LIQUID PAST** Since the days of Schiaparelli, astronomers have wondered if there was water on Mars. In 2004 NASA's Opportunity rover found evidence strongly suggesting a watery past for the planet. At an outcropping dubbed "El Capitan," the rover found parallel laminations in the surface, fine mineral layers usually laid down by settling water, as well as cavities called vugs, formed when salt crystals form in briny water, then fall out or dissolve.

Even more compelling were the BB-size spherules in the picture at left, also found at El Capitan, which NASA scientists dubbed "blueberries." Such spherules are formed either by volcanic activity or by minerals accreting under water, but the way the blueberries are mixed randomly through the rock strongly suggests they were not volcanic in origin. Chemical analyses show El Capitan to be rich in hematite, a sulfate known to form in the presence of water.

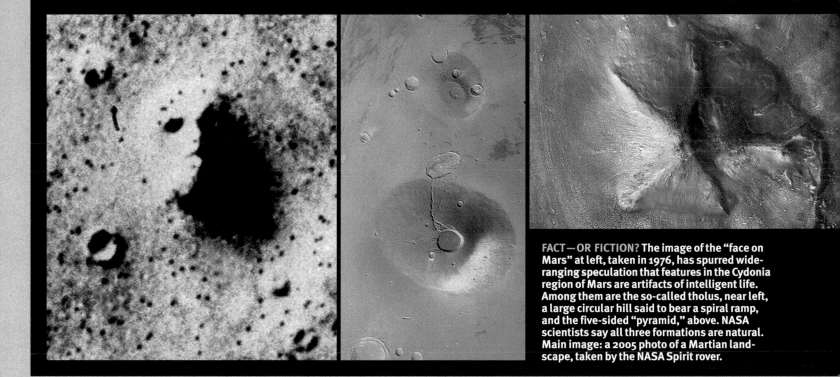

FACT—OR FICTION? The image of the "face on Mars" at left, taken in 1976, has spurred wide-ranging speculation that features in the Cydonia region of Mars are artifacts of intelligent life. Among them are the so-called tholus, near left, a large circular hill said to bear a spiral ramp, and the five-sided "pyramid," above. NASA scientists say all three formations are natural. Main image: a 2005 photo of a Martian land-scape, taken by the NASA Spirit rover.

detailed examination of surface anomalies on the planet. It all began when NASA's Viking 1 probe, orbiting the planet, photographed a large feature in the Cydonia region in the northern hemisphere. A NASA press release noted that the feature, which scientists believed to be a mesa rising above the surface, bore an amusing resemblance to a human face—and the Mars theorists were off to the races.

The notion that the "face on Mars"—which has a slightly leonine cast—is an artifact of an ancient intelligent civilization was popular-ized by Richard C. Hoagland, a writer and space theorist with a fertile imagination. In his 1987 book *The Monuments of Mars,* Hoagland advanced the theory that the "face" was only one part of a vast complex in the Cydonia region; he also argues that nearby surface features included pyramids and the ruins of a city. (Interested? Check out Hoagland's theories at *www.enterprisemission.com.)*

Pictures of the "face" taken by more recent NASA missions have confirmed that it is simply a mesa, and that its likeness to a human was merely a trick of the light. One might assume that these photographs would persuade the believers in Cydonian splendor to abandon their theories. But one would be wrong. The photos, they argue, are a cover-up, only one part of a vast conspiracy to keep the truth about alien civilizations from man. But credit Hoagland, who maintains an extensive speaking schedule, an ongoing series of publications and a popular, advertiser-supported website, with this feat of discovery: on the arid surface of Mars, he has found gold.

■ **The feature, which scientists believed to be a mesa rising above the surface, bore an amusing resemblance to a human face**

## 4

# Mind and Matter

66 Physical concepts are free creations of the human mind, and are not, however it may seem, uniquely determined by the external world. 99 —Albert Einstein

# Your Eyes Are Heavy ...

The power of suggestion is potent indeed: scientists have documented that yawning is highly contagious, but extensive tests have been unable to explain why. Although meditation and the entering of trance states has long been a practice in many religions, the man who first harnessed the power of suggestion to hypnotize subjects was Austrian physician Franz Mesmer (1734-1815). Before marveling 18th century European audiences, he showed his power to influence the behavior of those he put under his spell—a process soon dubbed "mesmerizing." Mesmer believed his work tapped into a natural magnetic flow in the body, which he termed "animal magnetism." In the 19th century Mesmer's work was researched more thoroughly, and the term hypnosis was created, drawn from the Greek *hypnos,* god of sleep. But even as science explored the suggestibility of the human mind, entertainers and charlatans hijacked hypnosis, and the practice became associated more with silly spectacles than with serious science: watch Dad imitate a chicken!

Hypnotism is often incorrectly viewed as the exertion of one person's will over another's. More accurately, it can be defined as a trance state that is characterized by relaxation, elevated imagination, lowered inhibitions and extreme suggestibility. Hypnosis appears to bypass a subject's conscious mind, where inhibition dwells, and engages the subconscious, more intuitive mind. Studies of brain waves show that lower-frequency waves associated with sleep and dreaming are highly prevalent in hypnotized patients, while higher-frequency waves associated with wakefulness decline. In similar fashion, hypnosis causes a decline in activity in the left lobe of the cerebral cortex, which controls logic and reason, even as it elevates activity in the right lobe, the home of creative, impulsive thought.

In the 20th century, spurred by the growth of psychology and psychiatry, scientists began to take an increased interest in the subject. In the past 50 or 60 years, hypnosis has been widely used, with varying degrees of success, in behavioral therapy. Millions of Americans have employed hypnosis to stop smoking cigarettes or cut back on their eating.

Today hypnosis is less likely to be seen on a Las Vegas stage (although a few happy holdouts still make stooges cluck) and more likely to be found in a hospital. Since the early 1990s, hypnosis has increasingly been used in operating rooms as a substitute for or (more typically) as a complement to anesthesia. This application, now widely employed in Europe, stems in part from studies showing that hypnosedated patients suffer fewer side effects than fully sedated ones do—reducing such postoperative woes as nausea, fatigue, lack of coordination and cognitive impairment.

Meanwhile, studies using advanced scanning technology have shed additional light on how hypnosis works to block pain. In a 2004 report in the journal *Regional Anesthesia and Pain Medicine,* Dr. Sebastian Schulz-Stuebner of the University of Iowa reported that subjects' brain scans showed that the brain's cerebral cortex was not

RELAX ... A hypnotist practices his craft in the early 1960s. Long regarded as little more than a parlor trick, hypnotism has proved to be useful in behavioral therapy. It is now being used as a complement to anesthesia in hospital operating rooms

affected under hypnosedation: the "ouch" message wasn't making it past the midbrain and into consciousness.

In the U.S., more doctors are using hypnosis for procedures in which sedation is inappropriate or patients are allergic to anesthetics. Yet not even the most enthusiastic proponents of hypnosedation suggest it can replace anesthesia entirely. For one thing, not every-

body can be hypnotized; to oversimplify, one must be open to the process first. Some 60% of patients are hypnotizable to an extent; an additional 15%, highly so. The rest seem to be unresponsive.

Research into hypnoliteracy—the process by which writers and editors scheme to induce stupefaction in readers—is just beginning. But if you're feeling very sleepy, dear reader ... our magic is working.

# The Science of Psi

"I'm totally convinced it exists," Daryl Bem says of psi, the name used by academic researchers for extrasensory perception (ESP), telepathy and other forms of anomalous cognition. That is striking because Bem is not a fan of *The X-Files*. He holds a doctorate in psychology, is on the faculty at Cornell University and is a former instructor at both Harvard and Stanford universities. More important, he began his research aiming to prove that ESP is bunk.

Bem's conversion came about in the early 1990s, when he began an investigation into dozens of previous studies of psychic ability. All of them consisted of what psi researchers call Ganzfeld tests—German for "whole field"—in which a receiver is subjected to sensory deprivation and then asked to select one image from a group of four that a "sender" is viewing at another location and trying to telegraph mentally. Selecting only the research that had adhered to the most rigorous methods, Bem combined the results and subjected them to a sophisticated statistical analysis. The conclusion astounded him: while the laws of chance would predict that participants would select the right image about 25% of the time, the average Ganzfeld test subject was correct about 34% of the time. Some groups of test takers did even better: appearing to confirm a long-held suspicion that individuals with creative personalities are more likely to have psychic abilities, art students chose the right image half the time, and music students' success rate was almost 75%.

Even without the best results, the 34% success rate shocked the academic community. A deviation of 9% from an expected outcome is, to a statistician, enormous. Bem calculated the odds of his findings' occurring by chance to be less than 1 in 1 billion. Indeed, the statistical indication that something other than chance governed these results is far less ambiguous than the lower threshold of proof that is widely accepted to show, for example, that aspirin can benefit people with heart trouble. Nor was Bem alone in his interpretation of the numbers. Robert Rosenthal, then chairman of Harvard's psychology department, said at the time, "The statistical evidence in Bem's analysis is quite clear to me ... there is a phenomenon there that does require explaining."

So, what's the explanation? Alas, this is where the wheels come off the wagon for many scientists looking for a rational foundation for stories about telepathy and ESP. No law of current physics or biology can explain how one human brain might communicate with another, except through the five senses we all learned about in elementary school. But serious scientists—at the Princeton Engineering Anomalies Research Center, the Society for Psychical Research in London and the Koestler Institute at the University of Edinburgh, among others—are working hard to find such avenues.

One outcome plaguing efforts to transform psi into science is the so-called experimenter effect, which consistently shows that identical experiments, conducted once by a scientist inclined to believe in ESP and a second time by an investigator who is skeptical about it, will yield contradictory results. The believer will get encouraging data, whereas the skeptic will find evidence that ESP doesn't exist.

For scientists who prize open-mindedness as much as orthodoxy, however, the numbers don't lie. "You may not think it's psi," Bem says of the statistical evidence, "but something other than chance is happening." Bem, an amateur magician since he was a teenager (don't wince: magicians are often rigorous skeptics), reflects that "a lot of us went into the business seeking magic, and I guess we are still looking for it. Wouldn't it be nice if we didn't have to fake it?"

**PSI TRY ESP testers often use five symbols printed on "Zener cards," named for psychologist Karl Zener**

# Seeking Kids—and Headlines

"You can't imagine the desperation you feel when your child is missing," says Marc Klaas. "Your every thought, every emotion, every breath is devoted to only one thing—finding that child and bringing her home." Klaas is speaking from bitter experience: on the evening of Oct. 1, 1993, his 12-year-old daughter Polly was abducted at knifepoint from their home in Petaluma, Calif. Within a matter of days, local police had partnered with federal agencies to search for the girl, more than 4,000 volunteers had enlisted in the hunt, and national media attention had been trained on the small Sonoma County town, creating a frenzied atmosphere.

"I was frantic," Klaas says today, looking back from a perspective of 13 years. "For weeks, I slept as little as possible or not at all, and every waking moment was spent trying to get Polly back. I would go out with search parties, talk to reporters, redo interviews with the police, around the clock." Amid the media circus, Klaas was contacted repeatedly by individuals operating outside the normal law-enforcement system: psychics who seek to aid the police in criminal investigations, especially those related to missing children.

"I had never been a believer in things like ESP," Klaas says, "but as the days ticked by, I became willing to gamble on any chance of getting Polly back, no matter how remote." The visionaries who began knocking on the Klaas' door also offered an infusion of something he was running out of: hope. "The police kept hedging their bets," Klaas

**SCARS Since the 1993 murder of his daughter Polly, above, Marc Klaas has become an activist for the families of missing children—and a skeptic of police psychics**

recalls, "saying that all they could promise was to do their best. But several psychics straight-out promised they would get Polly back."

To Klaas' frustration, local police and federal agents dismissed the offers. "They had no interest in hearing about any leads that came from a psychic," Klaas says. "At one point, we got a very specific tip that Polly was being held on a nearby farm. The owner refused to let his property be searched, which only made me more certain that this was for real, but the police wouldn't even try to get a warrant. So I had to enlist a group of volunteers to come with me. Since we weren't supposed to be there, we had to sneak onto the place after dark. When the owner realized we were there, he came out and confronted us with a shotgun."

It would be nice to report that Polly Klaas was found that night on the farm, bringing this sad story to a happy ending. And it would be satisfying to read that tips provided by psychics contributed to that resolution. But neither is the case. "The police were right," Klaas now says of the information provided by psychics. "It was all nonsense. The psychics kept saying things like, 'I see rolling green hills alongside a road, near a small brook.' You know what? That describes about three-quarters of the state of California. They would say, 'I see a steep ravine off to the side of the road.' But criminal profilers who were working on Polly's case later told me that leaving a body in a low-lying area along a remote stretch of highway is a pattern in child-abduction cases."

Although the psychics were right about the wooded area near a road, they were wrong about the ravine. On Dec. 4, 1993, eight weeks after her abduction, Polly's remains were found near the top of a hill, not far from her home. Her murderer—a drifter and sex offender named Richard Allen Davis, who is now on death row in San Quentin State Prison—had dragged her up an embankment before killing her.

"After it was over," Klaas remembers, "I looked back and realized that about half the psychics we heard from had tried to get money out of us. They didn't call it a fee but would promise to get our daughter back for us if we would pay their 'expenses.' The other half were looking for publicity, rather than money." A few months later, when Klaas watched a television interview with a member of this latter group—a person who had made several predictions about the case, all of which turned out to be wrong—and heard her claim to have "solved" the case, he became physically ill. "I was astounded," he now recalls. "She was using this tragedy, my daughter's nightmarish death, for her own benefit."

Klaas' story is likely to disappoint some readers, for in recent years, a raft of books and movies, as well as the TV shows *Medium, Missing* and *Psychic Detectives,* have created the impression that clairvoyants and seers are a legitimate part of criminal investigations, if only as a tool used in exceptional cases. But a variety of law-enforcement sources contacted by TIME dispute this notion.

Allison DuBois, the real-life psychic who is the inspiration for the NBC crime drama, *Medium* (in which a character of the same name is played by Patricia Arquette), is a case in point. In her 2005 book, *Don't Kiss Them Good-bye,* she repeatedly claims to have assisted the legendary Texas Rangers in child-abduction cases. Consistent with a pattern observed in other psychics making such claims, DuBois does not provide the names of the victim, the alleged perpetrator or the investigators with whom she claims to have worked. Yet when contacted by TIME, Texas Rangers spokesman Tom Vinger said, "The answer is an unequivocal no. Nobody here remembers Allison DuBois consulting on any investigation. We don't work with psychics. We have not, do not and do not plan to." DuBois, through her representatives, declined to speak with TIME for this book.

Special Agent Ann Todd, a spokesman for the FBI, while not willing to comment on DuBois specifically, echoes Vinger. "As a matter of policy, we don't work with psychics," she explains. "Nor do we allow them to participate in federal investigations." She goes on to say that "to my knowledge, not a single case has ever been closed or a single conviction ever obtained with evidence from a psychic."

Robert O'Brien, senior director of the Missing Children's Division at the National Center for Missing and Exploited Children and a retired FBI special agent, concurs. "I am not aware of any cases where information provided by a psychic led to the location of a missing child." On the contrary, O'Brien says, "information provided by psychics ... frequently promotes angst and fear among the victims' families and has dismal chances of success." Calls to police departments in New York City, Boston, Chicago and Los Angeles yielded similar answers.

The popular fascination with notions of police psychics ignores several glaring problems. "If somebody claiming to be a psychic produced information they couldn't possibly have known, like the location of a body," O'Brien notes, "an experienced investigator would

ROLE MODEL Psychic Allison DuBois, left, inspired the character played by Patricia Arquette, right, with co-star Miguel Sandoval, on TV's *Medium*

immediately consider that person a suspect in the crime." Todd says that "information developed by people who claim to be able to read minds or foretell the future is not the kind of witness statement you could use to get a warrant, and would probably be inadmissable as evidence during trial. And if police or prosecutors were found to have used such material, it would certainly be grounds for an appeal."

Even skeptics who ridicule astrology as a pseudoscience admit that people's attraction to it is harmless—a guilty pleasure at worst. But Klaas feels that would-be crime-solving psychics occupy a different category. "They prey upon people who are terrified," he says. "At their worst, they can distract police and obstruct investigations, and they waste time when there is no time to waste. They want credibility and legitimacy, because the attention makes them more marketable for books, speaking engagements and private consultations."

Klaas concludes by saying, "Everybody wants the answers that psychics claim to provide—that their deceased parents are O.K., or that their missing child is coming home. But sometimes, the truth turns out not to be the answer you want—and in other cases, there is no answer at all. It's difficult enough to face that reality without somebody trying to make a buck by offering you false hope." Tales of psychic crime fighters may make for gripping TV shows—but they have yet to gain traction with real-life law-enforcement agencies.

# Connected at Birth

At a glance, Jim Lewis and Jim Springer, who met for the first time in the mid-1980s, didn't seem to have much in common — beyond a shared given name and the same birthday. The two men, who had been brought together as part of a University of Minnesota study on identical twins who had been separated at birth, didn't even look very much alike, with contrasting hair-styles and ways of dressing.

Yet after a few minutes of conversation, the men (who were adopted by separate Ohio families four weeks after they were born) realized that their lives were unnerving mirror images: both had married and divorced women named Linda, married second wives named Betty and named their first sons James Allan and James Alan, respectively. Both men drove Chevrolets (the same model and shade of blue), smoked the same brand of cigarettes and enjoyed the same hobby — woodworking, which led them to build identical circular benches around trees in their backyards, 45 miles apart. Both suffered from recurring headaches at the same hour of the day. And both had dogs named Toy.

This list of coincidences seems to strain credulity, and a skeptic might argue that the two Jims were at least raised in similar environments. But how to explain Oskar Stohr and Jack Yufe? Separated a few months after their mother gave birth, one boy was raised a Catholic in Nazi Germany and joined the Hitler Youth. The other was raised a Jew, living on a kibbutz in Israel after the war. But when the men were reunited in 1991, they sported identical thin mustaches, wire-rimmed glasses and blue, two-pocket shirts with shoulder epaulets. The brothers, who walked with similar gaits and loved spicy foods, also shared a long list of signature idiosyncrasies: reading books and magazines from back to front, wearing rubber bands on their right wrists and flushing toilets before each use.

Since Stohr and Yufe were raised in environ-ments that were starkly dissimilar, we seem to be left with genetics to explain their common traits. But because science has yet to isolate a gene for reading books backward, many observers instinctively look for another rationale.

The psychic bond that twins seem to share has been documented extensively and is understood almost not at all. Sonograms often show twins seeming to hold hands or cling together in the womb. Mothers often report that infant twins sleeping in separate rooms will lie in the same positions, roll over at the same time and be disturbed by nightmares simultaneously.

Twins in school are sometimes accused by teachers of cheating on exams because of their tendency to get the same scores, with the same questions wrong due to the same incorrect answers. The scores of Identical twins on IQ tests are often closer together than the scores of one person who takes the test twice. As evidence of the unseen connection between twins mounts, mainstream science is paying far more attention to the subject.

The most puzzling and hotly disputed aspect of the twin connection is the phenomenon of "sympathetic pain," in which one twin claims to feel the discomfort of another, even when they are separated by great distances. A famous example of such "twin synchronicity" involves Norris and Ross McWhirter, the co-founding editors of the *Guinness Book of World Records*. Until his death in 2004, Norris claimed to have doubled over and collapsed on the evening of Nov. 27, 1975. Members of his family thought he was suffering a heart attack, but doctors could find nothing wrong with him. Hours later, word arrived that Ross , a foe of the Irish Republican Army, had been shot to death by IRA gunmen at his London home — at the moment Norris was writhing in pain 30 miles away.

**MIRRORS Many aspects of twin behavior simply defy our current understanding of the laws of nature**

# Remote Patrol

"From these experiments we conclude that ... a channel exists whereby information about a remote location can be obtained by means of an as yet unidentified perceptual modality." In 1974, these words sent shock waves through the scientific community, because they appeared not in a supermarket tabloid but in the widely respected science journal *Nature*. The article, published under the bland title "Information Transmission Under Conditions of Sensory Shielding," recounted tests conducted by two scholars at the Stanford Research Institute, Russell Targ and Harold Puthoff, that seemed to document a previously unknown ability in some test subjects to "see" events taking place at great distances.

While Targ and Puthoff cautioned that this ability, which they called remote viewing, appeared to be rare and yielded very general images even in the best of cases, their methodology adhered to the strictest scientific protocols. Among the general public, the news briefly piqued the interest of peeping Toms and insider traders. But it inspired more serious—and more lasting—curiosity from another group of people whose business it is to figure out what's going on in places that are supposed to be safe from prying eyes, the U.S. intelligence community. Beginning in the mid-1970s and continuing for another 20 years, an array of secret U.S. agencies began to dabble in remote viewing. Under code names like Scanate and Inscom (at the CIA), Sun Streak and Center Lane (at the Defense Intelligence Agency) and Project Stargate (at the National Security Agency), spymasters recruited scientists and psychics in hopes of peering behind the Iron Curtain.

Unfortunately, much of what the subjects came up with was interesting but so vague as to be meaningless. And some of it was complete nonsense. Sometimes, though, the government's remote viewers developed information that was stunning in its detail and accuracy, as documents declassified in the past few years reveal. Working from a bungalow at Maryland's Fort Meade (the NSA's headquarters) and a lab in Menlo Park, Calif., viewers described a Chinese nuclear test in Lop Nur and a Russian submarine being built in Severodvinsk. They located a downed Soviet fighter in the Zaïrean jungle, providing an intelligence coup when U.S. agents reached the plane before the Soviets did and were able to snatch much of its sophisticated electronic equipment. And they described accurately the location of a U.S. Navy plane that had crashed in the North Carolina wilderness. Government viewers also helped smoke out an eavesdropping post near the U.S. embassy in Moscow.

But the stakes were perhaps highest in 1987 when the remote viewers were asked for clues about the identity of a possible mole within the CIA. The subjects envisioned a man who lived in a lavish home near Washington, owned an expensive foreign car and was close to a woman from Latin America. The information was filed away and forgotten until February 1994, when Aldrich Ames—who lived in a palatial house in Arlington, Va., drove a Jaguar and was married to a Colombian woman—was arrested on charges of having spied for the Russians for more than a decade. The case also highlights the problems of working with even the best information from remote viewers: it often comes into sharpest focus only in retrospect.

"I see a river ..."

"I see a city all around the tower ..."

## "I see a tower ..."

VISIONS In remote-viewing tests the information provided is often general and large scale: a viewer trying to identify Paris might sense only three main features: the Eiffel Tower, the Seine and a cluster of surrounding structures. The inset images, taken from a 1978 test of remote viewing, show the Palo Alto, Calif., airport tower and the sketch drawn by a viewer who was trying to visualize it from a few miles away

What's also perfectly clear in hindsight is the politically explosive nature of enlisting government agencies to flirt with the paranormal. When Stargate and related projects became public knowledge in 1995, it was an an invitation for skeptics to heap ridicule on public servants, while those with an unwavering belief in otherworldly power, including some fundamentalist Christian groups, interpreted the stories to mean that their tax dollars were underwriting occult activities. Congress quickly killed the program, but not before commissioning a study to see what had been achieved.

Among the report's authors were one of the nation's leading statisticians, Jessica Utts, and one of its most eminent professional skeptics of the paranormal, psychologist Ray Hyman. Together, they determined that the $20 million spent on remote viewing had been a dubious investment—with one caveat: Hyman acknowledged that the "hit" rates in lab experiments were statistically impossible to ascribe to dumb luck, while Utts wrote that "using the standards applied to any other area of science, the case for psychic functioning has been scientifically proven."

# Movers and Shakers

All of us must harbor some suspicion that psychokinesis—the ability to manipulate the physical world through mental effort alone—is real, because we've all tried it. Who hasn't closed their eyes and urged a car that wouldn't start, "Come on, baby!" As old as the Bible (the second *Book of Kings* tells of the prophet Elisha's willing an iron ax head that had sunk in the Jordan River to float) and as current as cutting-edge research, psychokinesis represents the best and worst of attempts to make sense of paranormal phenomena.

Performers like Israeli-born mentalist Uri Geller have proved beyond any doubt their ability to induce gasps in audiences by appearing to bend spoons and melt metallic objects onstage, seeming to use only the force of their concentration. But there has never been a single demonstration under scientifically controlled conditions that bears out such claims. Not one. And more than a few of the claimants have been exposed as ... well, movers and fakers.

Unfortunately, the cynicism generated by such activities spills over onto serious attempts to investigate psychokinesis (the term comes from the Greek words for mind and movement), or PK. "There are a lot of charlatans and frauds in a field like this," Robert Jahn, director of the Princeton Engineering Anomalies Research (PEAR) lab and dean emeritus of the university's engineering department, says wearily. "Naturally some people are wary of what we do." Indeed, disbelieving academics quip that PK research definitely proves the power of "mind over data," and professional skeptic James Randi has been known to extend to audiences the invitation, "Everyone who believes in psychokinesis, raise my hand." Yet PEAR and similar facilities have confirmed the existence of strange effects upon what are supposed to be random events, and those findings are not so easy to laugh off.

Scientific research into PK was begun in the 1920s by Duke University researcher J.B. Rhine and was continued later at other institutions, focusing on the role of "intention" in throws of the dice. Participants were asked to mentally influence the numbers that came up on each roll. More than 100 separate studies—covering 2.6 million throws by more than 2,500 people—yielded a small but consistent statistical edge in favor of the outcome the participants were trying to achieve. (Casino managers can breathe easy: the difference amounts to 2 rolls in 10,000, a much smaller proportion than the house edge in craps, but much larger than mathematicians say can be attributed to chance in a trial of this size.)

The research was resumed at PEAR in the 1990s, with computerized random-number generators standing in for the tumbling dice. More than 800 experiments yielded an intriguing (and consistent) result: human intention apparently not only had the same effect on the computers as it had on the dice but also did so by almost precisely the same proportion. Indeed, in 1995 no less an archskeptic than Carl Sagan cited this finding as one of three claims of paranormal phenomenon that he felt warranted serious scientific investigation. "If you get your mind in resonance with the processor," explains Jahn, "it will show a preference for following your desire."

Fair enough, but why? A promising theory that seeks to explain how our thoughts might influence the world around us is being formulated by Nobel laureate physicist Brian Josephson. "We think it's related to the Einstein-Podolsky-Rosen paradox," the Briton says, referring to a puzzle of subatomic physics in which two particles,

**Psychokinesis, like hypnotism, has been the subject of both popular entertainment and serious laboratory research. Here are some scenes from its history, left to right:**
**URI GELLER** The entertainer, left, made a huge splash in the 1970s with his seeming ability to bend metal objects like keys, but laboratory tests have never substantiated his claims
**DUKE STUDIES** The first reputable tests of ESP and psychokinesis were begun by psychologist J.B. Rhine at Duke University in 1927; here J.G. Pratt, at left, and Jack Bevan are trying to move dice
**LITTLE LARIATS** A group of cowboys takes part in a 1999 experiment to see if they can move pieces of string with their minds. No roundup ensued
**FRAUD?** Polish medium Stanislawa Tomczyk demonstrates psychokinesis in the presence of investigator Julien Ochorowicz, circa 1910; the photograph was very likely manipulated
**MR. MAGNET** Liew Thow Lin of Malaysia, top right, says he is a "human magnet," whose skin attracts metal and holds it. Malaysian researchers said his skin creates a suction effect; we're dubious

separated by large distances in space and time, can be observed to act in tandem with one another.

Attempting to translate this quandary into layman's terms, Jahn theorizes that "consciousness can insert information into its environment." He goes on to suggest that consciousness, which we often think of in terms of particles—the individual mind, localized in time and space—may also act like a wave, diffused across time and space. The same duality (in which light, for example, behaves like both a particle and a wave) is commonly observed in quantum physics, where intersecting wave fields form resonating patterns. Jahn believes that psychokinesis (and many other forms of paranormal phenomena) may result from a poorly understood human ability to tap into such fields. PK could be the resonance between human consciousness and an object; telepathy might come from the waves of two minds overlapping each other, and so on. Atoms themselves are only constructs of the mind, says Jahn. "And our heads are TV sets that capture and tune in the consciousness waves out of which our universe is built."

NOSTRADAMUS

# Father of the Future?

Yes, Nostradamus could see into the future. A physician and astrologer in 16th century France, he was among the first to recognize the potential of a new invention—the printing press, then barely 30 years old—to make (if not tell) fortunes. And he proceeded to make his.

In the 1550s Michel de Nostredame, who signed important documents with the Latinized version of his name, Nostradamus, began publishing a series of books that divulged jealously guarded trade secrets: formulas for cosmetics and the recipes for potions mixed by pharmacists. A canny promoter, the aspiring writer boosted demand by sending free copies of his books to the royal courts and religious leaders of Europe. Since physicians and psychics were thought to be closely related at that time, he was a natural choice when the wealthy and powerful needed advice about the future. He hit pay dirt in 1559, when he penned the following verse:

*The young lion will overcome the older one,*
*On the field of combat in single battle,*
*He will pierce his eyes through a golden cage,*
*Two wounds made one, then he dies a cruel death*

Months later France's King Henry II staged a mock joust with the Count of Montgomery, six years his junior; both their shields were emblazoned with lions. In a final pass, the Count lost control of his lance, and it passed through the eye slit of Henry's golden helmet, splintering into shards as it went. Two large slivers penetrated deep into Henry's brain. He died 10 days later.

With that, Nostradamus was off to the races. Every crowned head in Europe sought his advice, and he began devoting himself full time to staring into a brass bowl filled with water and conjuring visions of the future. At this he proved exceedingly adept, for he had all the important skills of a professional seer.

First, he maneuvered for maximum wiggle room. If Nostradamus knew that a patron did not speak French, he would reply in that tongue, although Latin was Europe's common language at the time. Eschewing a professional scribe, he used only his own deliberately inscrutable handwriting.

Second, he kept matters vague, answering questions he hadn't been asked rather than those he had. His predictions make the Oracle at Delphi seem a model of clarity. And he was cagey about names, often using code words with multiple meanings. His "New City" could be Naples, Villanova or, centuries later, New York City.

Even so, many passages he set down in the last 10 years of his life seem eerily evocative (if not predictive) of the French Revolution, the rise of Napoleon, World War II, the atom bomb, the AIDS pandemic and many more. Consider this passage:

*The ancient work will be accomplished,*
*And from the roof evil ruin will fall on to the great man.*
*Being dead, they will accuse an innocent of the deed,*
*The guilty one hidden in the misty woods.*

These words resonate with those obsessed with John F. Kennedy's assassination—but also with those seeking predictions of the 1981 attempt on Pope John Paul II's life or the 1995 murder of Yitzhak Rabin. In each case, the vision came into focus only after the event. Another passage refers to someone (or something) named "Hister" as the focus of a great war in Europe involving Germany. Hitler, perhaps? Yet Hister could refer to the Danube River (the Greek name for which is "Ister"), across which Germany has fought many wars.

Finally, Nostradamus focused on life's eternals: kings, popes, wars and disasters. Thus his work never ages: it is a blank slate onto which a willing reader can project anything he wishes to see. But one prediction certainly came to pass: Nostradamus said, shortly before his death in 1566, that his posthumous fame would only grow. Good call!

FORESEEN? Readers claim to have found references to Napoleon, Hitler, the atom bombing of Japan and the 9/11 terrorist attacks on New York City in Nostradamus' works. At left, the seer and an early edition of his major work, *Les Prophecies.* Many of his predictions were based on his study of history and the work of prophets who preceded him

**MADAME BLAVATSKY** Born in Ukraine, the mystic and clairvoyant helped found the Theosophical Society in 1875 and helped bring many occult practices to a wide audience.

**EDGAR CAYCE** Hugely popular in the early 20th century, the "sleeping prophet" channeled his predictions from a trance state. A devotee of astrology and reincarnation, he anticipated many New Age beliefs.

**JEANE DIXON** The most popular astrologer and psychic in the U.S. for many years, she predicted John F. Kennedy's assassination, but her many failed predictions were far less publicized and are now generally forgotten.

# Mediums for the Masses

"How many times have you sensed the presence of somebody you love who has died?" asks television medium John Edward. "Gone from just thinking about them to the strong feeling that they were thinking about you at that moment? That's a nearly universal human experience. The truth is, I'm just like anybody else, except this sensitivity is somewhat more developed in me. I'm unusual only in the respect that I can serve as a channel for other people to experience this, while most people can do it only for themselves."

Celebrity seers—individuals who claim they have the ability to peer into the future or converse with the spirits of the dead—have good reasons to foresee a bright future for their trade. A 2005 Gallup poll found that half of all Americans believe in ESP, while more than 40% are convinced that haunted houses exist and about a third put their faith in astrology, clairvoyance and ghosts. Little wonder, then, that our mass media are increasingly crowded with mass mediums like John Edward.

This charismatic clairvoyant first found fame with *Crossing Over with John Edward,* a show that debuted in 1999 on the Sci Fi network, in which he claimed to channel deceased loved ones for members of his studio audience. In March 2006 he launched a new show on the WE network, *John Edward Cross Country,* a kind of psychic road trip in which he visits the bereaved in their homes.

"Do you know what my biggest goal is?" Edward asks. "To make people realize they don't need me. To make people understand that they don't need a medium. On some level, we all sense the truth. Sometimes we see it vaguely, or in a hazy outline; sometimes we only suspect it. But we all have the capacity inside of us to grasp it."

To watch Edward at work on TV is to be dazzled by the frequency with which he "hits" on intimate details of the lives of dead people he never met. And yet there has never been a successful test under scientifically rigorous conditions of his ability (or that of any other seer) to communicate with the dead. So how does Edward do it?

Some stage performers can evoke the same responses as Edward, though they lay no claim to possessing psychic powers. One is British magician Ian Rowland, who calls himself a "mind reader and mind motivator." Rowland has repeatedly demonstrated techniques that can be used to cajole identifying details out of the people he speaks to, while appearing to have come up with the information himself.

One powerful tool is known as "cold reading," which Rowland describes as "an interactive psychological technique that allows you to influence how someone else perceives you." Cold readers pose a series of questions and suggestions shaped by the subject's replies. "Magicians use this all the time to create the appearance of mind reading," Rowland explains, "but it is also very useful for police conducting interrogations, sales people who want to be the customer's best friend, or anybody who needs to shape perception."

Practitioners will often begin by uttering a generality: "I sense an older father figure here," eliciting a response that leads him to the next question. "I'm getting that his death resulted from a problem in his chest" is a statistically sound guess that could cover everything from lung cancer or emphysema to a heart attack. Should the subject answer no, the cold reader will often say, "Well, we'll get back to that," and quickly change course. It's a sophisticated form of the game Twenty Questions, during which the subject, anxious to hear from the dead, seldom realizes that he, not the medium or the departed, is supplying the answers. "People shouldn't concentrate on the hits," explains Rowland. "What gives it away are the misses."

"There are people who are never going to believe in this," Edward admits . "And I don't begrudge them their skepticism. But for me, this is real. I believe in it. You may think that I'm mistaken, and that's fair. But if you really listen, I don't think you'll come away with the sense that I'm making this up. My first experience with messages from people who had left this life came in 1987, after my mother died. I got a powerful, overwhelming feeling that her love for me was more than just a memory—that it still existed. That made a huge difference in coping with her loss and was the beginning of my belief that human consciousness survives physical death. So what I try to do now is educate and enlighten people—and maybe even entertain a little bit at the same time. Because all of those things add up to healing."

Is John Edward merely a talented showman, or can he genuinely communicate with the world beyond life? Rowland reserves judgment, pointedly refusing to accuse Edward of fraud. A 2001 TIME story cited a particpant on *Crossing Over* who made serious accusations that some portions of the show were staged; careful editing of film clips can add an enormous sense of drama to otherwise routine moments. As is the case with faith healers, it is difficult to draw a line: is Edward praying with his faithful—or preying upon them? He is a minister of sorts, offering consolation to people facing the loss of a beloved relative, and he conveys messages of forgiveness and love from the dearly departed to those who need it most. For those who choose to believe in his powers, that is a blessing. Like a master chef, he cooks up what we all crave in times of need: chicken soup for the soul. Just don't go checking the ingredients too carefully

# Sneak Previews of Fate

Will I be rich? Married? Happy? When will I die? Few human fantasies are more common than the wish to see into the future. The mechanics of fortune telling take many forms. Some believe our fate is written into our bodies. Don't laugh: today we scoff at phrenology but swear by DNA. Some believe fate can be divined—revealed by the occult tools of the trade shown here

**TAROT CARDS:** Rich with archetypal images—the Lovers, Death, the Sun, the Fool—the tarot deck is an ancient tool of divination; some 20th century psychologists like C.G. Jung believed the cards refer to aspects of the unconscious. The earliest extant decks date to 15th century Italy, but it was not until the 19th century that the use of the cards to tell fortunes became widespread. The Rider-Waite deck, first published in 1909, is the most familiar version.

The Fool

**CLEROMANCY:** Attempts to predict one's fortune by casting bones, dice, sticks or other charms are common in many cultures and draw on the notion that the random nature of the event reflects or channels forces prevailing at the time of the toss—what modern science refers to as synchronicity. China's ancient *I Ching* text codifies this widely used form of divination. A Zulu diviner casts charms, above.

**PHRENOLOGY AND PALM READING:** There is an undeniable attraction to the notion that our fates are reflected in our bodies, although Freud was thinking of gender when he declared that "biology is destiny."

Phrenology, a pseudo-science popular in the 19th century, posited that the shape of one's head reflected the shape of the brain, revealing one's character traits.

Palm reading, or chiromancy, although also derided by scientists, remains popular, perhaps because of its eternally fascinating focus: me, me, me!

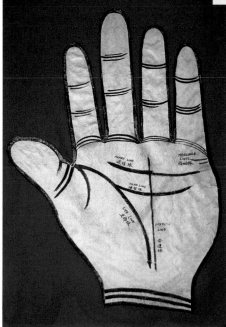

**CRYSTAL BALLS:** The use of globes of crystal or black glass to evoke visions of the future is very ancient, if now primarily associated with the Gypsies of Eastern Europe. Some historians believe Celtic Druids used crystals, or "shew stones," for prophecy. More recent seers, like Nostradamus, preferred to use hydromancy, gazing into a bowl of water, to see into the future. In most cases, the crystal or body of water is not regarded as magical in itself; rather, it is an aid to inducing a trance state in the seer. The "magic mirror" familiar from the tale of Snow White is another medium used by clairvoyants.

**OUIJA BOARD:** Modeled on alphabetical tablets used in 19th century séances, this do-it-yourself hotline to the spirit world was introduced in the 1890s and reached a zenith of popularity in the 1920s. Scientists say the movements of the planchette are controlled by the unconscious ideomotor effect, much like the swerves of a dowser's rod.

# In Asia, Mind Trumps Matter

Since the days when Europeans first encountered Asian cultures, the mystical practices of the East have amazed outsiders. Swamis, yogis, fakirs and gurus, it is said, can perform astonishing feats through mental discipline obtained by long years of practice: they can walk over live coals or lie on a bed of nails without injury. Many of the showpieces are carnival stunts rather than mystical marvels

**FIERY SOLES:** Like many Asian mystical practices, fire walking is not an end in itself; it is a symbol of the mind's ability to triumph over physical reality. Above, a young monk takes a stroll at the Nagatoro Fire Festival in Saitama, Japan, in 2004. Skeptics point out that the hot coals are often covered by insulating ash, and that wood ash is a very poor conductor of heat. It also helps that sensible fire walkers follow the age-old advice of New York City subway motormen: Step lively!

**SNAKE CHARMING:** This ancient street amusement is now dying out in India, its homeland. Its secrets: the poisonous snake, seemingly hypnotized by the music, is responding to the movement of the flute. The charmer sits just out of striking reach; some remove the fangs from their co-stars. Now stuntmen, charmers were once healers and magicians.

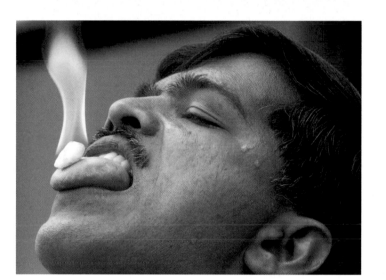

**FIRE EATING:** Hulikal Nataraju, from India's Miracle Research Center, displays a piece of burning camphor on his tongue during a 2004 event titled "Secrets of Miracles" in Bangalore, India. The event was organized to show students the science behind tricks used to cheat rural people. Real fire eaters do not use a protective gel; the dangerous art involves knowing that hot air rises—and keeping it rising!

**BED OF NAILS:** Like fire walking, this practice can thrill onlookers, but understanding the physics of the stunt takes away some of the "wow" factor. The trick is to use a large number of nails, thus distributing the body's weight among many points, ensuring no single nail will pierce the skin—even when a cinder block is placed on one's chest and shattered by a hammer. The most difficult aspect of the practice is learning to get into—and out of—the recumbent position safely.

# Powers of the Spirit

## 5

" We are not human beings having a spiritual experience. We are spiritual beings having a human experience. "

— Pierre Teilhard de Chardin

# A Flood of Conjecture

Behold Mount Ararat, whose summit, often draped in clouds, is believed by many to be the resting place of antiquity's most famous vessel, Noah's Ark. The tale of a great universal flood, sent by an angry God to punish a wicked world, is famously told in *Genesis,* the first book of the Old Testament, chapters 6 through 9. The biblical story says that the Ark came to rest on this mountain, which is located in Turkey, not far from the border of Iran.

But are the tales of the Old Testament intended to be literal fact, roadmaps to discovery? Or are they intended as parables, guideposts of spiritual insight? However readers choose to interpret the words of the Bible, one point is beyond dispute: modern-day science and technology—frequently pitted as adversaries of religion—have proved instead to be sources of illumination, clarifying the reality of stories that earlier generations might have written off as fables. Biblical archaeology is a respected and growing scientific discipline.

Thanks to satellite imagery, historians now believe they know the location of Ubar, once ruled by the Queen of Sheba but long buried beneath the sands of the Arabian desert. Satellite images also charted the lost course of the Pison River, one of four waterways the Bible says encircled the Garden of Eden. In 2000, Robert Ballard, the underwater explorer who located the remains of the *Titanic,* declared that his team had discovered the remains of a 7,000-year-old civilization that existed on the Turkish coast of the Black Sea before the region was inundated by a flood.

Geologists say the ancient civilizations of the Mediterranean were wracked by massive floods more than once in the millenniums before Christ. In fact, the story of a massively destructive ancient flood is common to many cultures, including Islam. The Koran identifies the resting place of the Ark as Al Judi, some 20 miles from Mount Ararat but in the same mountain range.

Accounts of the sighting of remains of the Ark on Ararat can be traced back to Roman times. Marco Polo claimed he saw the Ark on his journey through Turkey to Cathay in the late 15th century. More recently, seekers of the lost Ark have fixated on a location high on the slopes of Ararat, where a U.S. reconnaissance aircraft took a photo of a boat-shaped object in 1949. That photograph, dubbed the Mount Ararat Anomaly and classified for decades, was made public at the urging of scholar and Ark hunter Porcher Taylor in 1995. Believers and skeptics read this image very differently; some see it as the remains of an ancient vessel, whereas others say it shows natural features. The government of Turkey refused to allow permission for a proposed 2004 expedition to the site led by U.S. Ark hunter Daniel McGivern. Skeptical scientists note that the location of the anomaly, at some 14,000 ft. above sea level, is far too elevated to reflect the actual height of an ancient flood. Another fact complicates the search for the Ark: Byzantine Christians were known to have created life-size replicas of biblical artifacts, and objects located on Mount Ararat may be the remains of latter-day shrines, rather than original relics.

Meanwhile, other scientists say they have found remnants of a vessel resembling the Ark some 5,000 ft. up Al Judi—precisely where the Koran said they would be. Nearby were large drogue stones, used to stabilize ancient vessels. The search for the Ark continues, as new technologies bring ancient mysteries back from the dead.

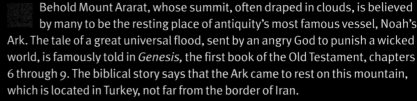

**TWO BY TWO** A painting by 18th century American artist Edward Hicks imagines the Ark, which biblical scholars estimate was some 450 ft. long

"As soon as the army had no more people to slay or to plunder ... Caesar gave orders that they should now demolish the entire city and Temple, but should leave ... so much of the wall as enclosed the city on the west side ... but for all the rest of the wall, it was so thoroughly laid even with the ground ... that there was left nothing to [indicate that Jerusalem] had ever been inhabited."

Josephus, the historian of Judaism, thus chronicled the destruction of the Second Temple by the Roman army in A.D. 70. This physical center of the Jewish universe was erected on the site of the First Temple, built by King Solomon on the spot where Abraham was said to have offered his son Isaac in sacrifice, only to have his hand stayed by an angel. That temple, which held the Ark of the Covenant and the Ten Commandments, was destroyed when the Jews were exiled into the Babylonian Captivity.

After the Romans pillaged the Second Temple, all that remained of Judaism's holiest site was one flank, facing to the west, of the retaining wall that had shored up the platform on which the temple sat. Built from stones up to 30 ft. long and weighing more than 50 tons each, this fragment of the temple's foundation, now called the Western Wall, is more than 100 ft. high and 16 ft. thick.

In the 20 centuries since the Second Temple was destroyed, the Western Wall has been partially buried and sometimes obscured by later construction. Only about 200 ft. of its quarter-mile length remains visible, but it has never ceased to be the melancholy object of Jewish longing for the restoration of an idealized past. Along the way it acquired a second name, al-Buraq, Arabic for "the Wall," and a religious significance every bit as profound for Muslims as for Jews. Islam teaches that Muhammad was borne by a winged horse from Mecca to Jerusalem in a single night during the year 620; he tethered the steed to this wall

# Waters of the Western Wall

and then ascended into the clouds with the angel Gabriel, who conducted the Prophet on a tour of both heaven and hell. This makes al-Buraq (and the Islamic shrine that sits above it, the Dome of the Rock) one of the holiest places in the Muslim world. Sadly, Middle East strife has made this site, central to two of the world's great religions, perhaps the single most contested patch of ground on the planet.

For today's adherents of both faiths, the Western Wall has acquired a new name: al-Mabka (Arabic for "the Place of Weeping"), or the Wailing Wall (a term coined by the British during their 19th century occupation of Jerusalem). Both refer to the belief, widely shared by Jews and Muslims, that God pays special attention to prayers spoken—or in the case of Jews, written on small pieces of paper and slipped between the wall's stones—at this place.

The tradition that miracles occur on this site, Temple Mount, dates back to biblical times, when Jewish lore holds that an angel named Bethesda descended from heaven and tapped the ground near the temple with a rod, causing water to spring forth. This water was later said to have healing powers, and its pools were the site of numerous miracles. *The Gospel of John* declares that Jesus healed a man "that had been eight and 30 years under his infirmity" here.

Bethesda's waters reportedly ran dry around the time of the Roman destruction of Jerusalem, but both Jewish and Christian fundamentalists believe the spring will begin gushing again in the days immediately preceding the end of the world. So it was with some interest that both scientists and religious scholars noted in July 2002 that water had begun to trickle down the Western Wall. Its source has yet to be identified.

**SHRINE** Observant Jews pray at the Western Wall. A famous pilgrim, Pope John Paul II, added his petition at this site when he visited the Holy Land in 2000, hoping to heal ancient religious divisions

# Riddles of a Sacred Text

Some believe every word in the Bible is true; some believe its stories are fables, written more to inspire than to serve as a road map for scientists; and many of us fall somewhere in between. Here are some enduring mysteries of the ancient volume

**GARDEN OF EDEN:** The three great Abrahamic religions—Judaism, Christianity, Islam—all adhere to the account of mankind's primeval home given in the Old Testament's *Book of Genesis*. But where was the garden located? *Genesis* says it was bounded by four major rivers: the Tigris, Euphrates, Pishon and Gihon. If the first two of these are the modern rivers of the same name, the location might be somewhere in today's Turkey, Iran or Iraq. The modern-day identities and locations of Pishon and Gihon are unknown; the two rivers are the subject of intense debate. Some scholars believe the land on which the garden rested is now submerged; other scholars believe the story of the garden is a religious metaphor and does not correspond to a geographic location.

**THE BIBLE CODE:** First advanced by three Israeli researchers, the theory that numeric messages are encoded in the Torah was popularized in the U.S. by Michael Drosnin's 1997 book *The Bible Code*. Scientists who have studied the claims are far from convinced. Numbers also play a major role in some forms of Kabbalah, the most mystical branch of Judaism.

**ARK OF THE COVENANT:** This conveyance was crafted by the early Jews to hold the tablets on which the Ten Commandments were written; it later held samples of the manna eaten by the Jews during their wanderings in the wilderness, as well as the rod of Moses' brother Aaron, which worked wonders against the Egyptians. The Old Testament gives clear specifications for the Ark; it was made of acacia wood and was roughly 2 ft. by 2 ft. by 4 ft. in size. The carved lintel at left, found at the ancient town of Capernaum on the Sea of Galilee, and dated to A.D. 200 to 300, shows what may be the Ark borne on wheels, but during their long wanderings the Jews carried it before them on poles thrust into two golden rings. Two cherubim were at its ends, facing each other. The Ark was enshrined in King Solomon's first temple in Jerusalem, but it was lost to history when the Babylonians destroyed the city and plundered the temple in 586 B.C.

**THE STAR OF BETHLEHEM:** What was the heavenly body that guided three Magi to the nativity site of Jesus? These wise men, judicial astronomers, were members of the Magi class of ancient Persia, a group charged with maintaining religion by consulting the heavens (a magus is a high priest and the root of our word magic). Modern-day astronomers have proposed a number of astral events that might be the basis for the story of the star, including several planetary conjunctions that occurred around 4 to 2 B.C. Halley's Comet was visible in 12 B.C., too early a date for Christ's birth.

IL VERO RITRATTO DEL SANTISSIMO SUDARIO DV TORINO

# Threads of Wonder

Since the Middle Ages multitudes have believed that a piece of linen enshrined in Turin, Italy, is the burial shroud that Jesus Christ left in the tomb when he rose from the grave. The 14-ft.-long, herringbone-twill cloth bears the image of a naked and bearded man about 6 ft. tall, hair in a loose ponytail, back apparently scourged with a multithonged whip, hands crossed modestly before him. This sheet, centuries of believers have agreed, once held Christ's body.

Centuries of skeptics have disagreed. One of the first universally accepted documentations of what we now know as the Shroud of Turin is a letter calling it a fraud. In 1389 Pierre d'Arcis, then Bishop

of Troyes, France, described a "twofold image of one man, that is to say, the back and the front ... impressed together with the wounds which he bore." The linen cloth had occupied a place of honor in a church in the tiny French town of Lirey since the 1350s; D'Arcis, who was writing to his Pope, noted that "although it is not publicly stated to be the true shroud of Christ, nevertheless this is ... noised abroad in private." This annoyed D'Arcis, who wrote that one of his predecessors had ascertained that "the image is cunningly painted ... a work of human skill and not miraculously wrought."

In 1998 an unexpected person—Turin's Anastasio Cardinal

**VENERATED, STUDIED, SAVED** Scenes in the life of the shroud:
1. The face of the image has long been said to be that of the crucified Christ
2. A 17th century engraving shows prelates and royals venerating the shroud, though the figure depicted only approximates the actual image
3. The unfurled shroud is 14 ft. in length, with a double image of the figure
4. Samples of the shroud were sent to three universities for carbon dating
5. The shroud is displayed in Turin in 1931. For purposes of preservation, the linen wrapping is shown to the public only on rare occasions
6. Firefighter Mario Trematore and a policeman carry the casket holding the shroud out of the Cathedral of San Giovanni in Turin when the building was ravaged by fire in April 1997. Trematore smashed through eight layers of bulletproof glass with a hammer to reach the shroud, which was undamaged

scientific tests on the shroud in 1978, but he refused to permit scientists to use their most reliable dating tool, carbon 14 testing, which was crucial to determining the fabric's age. Handkerchief-size samples needed to be cut out, which, to Ballestrero, was unthinkable for such a revered historical item. After technical improvements made it possible to use samples the size of postage stamps, however, the Cardinal allowed cuttings to be taken in 1997.

Testing was done simultaneously at the University of Arizona, Britain's Oxford University and Switzerland's Federal Institute of Technology in Zurich. Each laboratory received four unmarked samples: a shroud cutting and three control pieces, one dating from the 1st century. The samples were chemically cleaned, burned to produce carbon dioxide, catalytically converted into graphite and then tested for carbon 14 isotopes to fix the date by calculating the amount of radioactive decay. Only London's British Museum, which coordinated the testing, knew which samples were which.

Arizona physicist Douglas Donahue said that the three laboratories reached a "remarkable agreement," all estimating dates within 100 years of one another. Averaging of the data produced a 95% probability that the shroud originated between 1260 and 1380 and near absolute certainty that it dates from no earlier than 1200. Some Catholics held out the slim hope, however, that there was a scientific oversight and the shroud might be redated someday.

The dating dispute that long surrounded the shroud may have been settled, but the object remains as mysterious as ever. Whatever its age, it bears an inexplicable life-size image of a crucified body, which is uncannily accurate and looks just like a photographic negative—yet it was made centuries before photography was invented. Elaborate testing in 1988 failed to produce any agreed explanation of how the image, which is difficult to read from close up, could have been imprinted. There is, for instance, no evidence that it was painted—a setback for Bishop D'Arcis' view.

To many, the continuing mystery of how the shroud's image was formed is miracle enough. Intrigued by these inexplicable matters, visitors continue to flock to Turin to venerate the shroud, which was publicly displayed in 2000 and underwent cleaning and conservation work in 2002. As Turin cab driver Angelo Di Conza explained to TIME, "Until they prove how the image got there— and the technology to make such an image didn't exist in the 14th century—then I think the scientific question remains open."

Ballestrero, custodian of the shroud—weighed in on the side of the skeptics, calmly announcing that scientific testing had proved the yellowing fabric is only six or seven centuries old and could not have dated from the time of Jesus. Thus ended the most intense scientific study ever conducted on a Christian relic.

The findings pleased skeptics, yet the shroud saga is not a major embarrassment for the Roman Catholic Church. From the days of D'Arcis, the church refused to declare the cloth authentic but had allowed it to be venerated as an inspiration to prayer. The studies that finally discredited the supposed age of the shroud were conducted with the church's full blessing, in an unusual alliance between honest faith and objective science. When Pope John Paul II was informed of the negative report, he ordered, "Publish it."

Ballestrero had initially agreed to an extraordinary series of

CHIVALRY'S GOAL **In the tapestry *Vision of the Grail* (1890), Edward Burne-Jones showed the chalice guarded by angels, while the knights Galahad, Bors and Percival venerate it.**

**Below, the saga lives on: Rocco Zingaro di San Ferdinando, grand master of the Knights Templars in Italy, holds what he claims is the Holy Grail, a chalice found in a Coptic monastery in Egypt in 2005.**

**In the main picture, Placido Domingo sings in Wagner's *Parsifal* at the Metropolitan Opera, 1992**

# On the Trail of the Grail

The Holy Grail! The term has slipped the traces of its religious origins and become a synonym for any goal that seems elusive, if not illusory: a ballplayer's home-run title, a physicist's new atomic particle, a medical researcher's cure for cancer. Yet although the nature of the Grail itself has been portrayed in many different ways, we can trace the development of this perhaps apocryphal sacred artifact back to its origins—and the trail leads us not to the Middle East in the age of Christ, but to the Middle Ages in the age of chivalry.

The first clue is the term itself: originally spelled *graal,* it is an old French term, derived from Latin, that refers to a serving dish used in a meal. And this is indeed how the Grail was first pictured, in the poem *Perceval, le Conte du Graal,* written after A.D. 1181 by one of the finest of medieval poets, Chrétien de Troyes. In this unfinished work, the hero, the knight Perceval, is present at a royal feast at which a Communion wafer, symbolic of the Last Supper, is carried in a marvelous procession, borne in a sacred serving dish, the *graal.*

Chrétien de Troyes was one of literature's great mythmakers; like the Grail legend, his fanciful tales of King Arthur and his knights also continue to resonate in Western culture. The idea of the *graal* caught the fancy of a poet of the next generation, Robert de Boron; in his long poem *Joseph d'Arimathie,* the Grail takes the form by which it is best known, as the chalice that Christ drank from at the Last Supper. De Boron imagines that Joseph of Arimathea, the wealthy man of the Gospels whose tomb was used to house the body of Christ, caught some of the savior's blood in the chalice after the crucifixion, then took the sacred receptacle to England, where it was protected at Glastonbury by a secret society of knights, one of whom was Perceval.

The story of the Grail carried a deep resonance in the Middle Ages, for it incorporated two themes that animated chivalry: Christian symbolism and the notion of a quest for an elusive ideal. Soon the tale of the Grail had spread to Germany, in Wolfram von Eschenbach's *Parzival;* to Wales, in the *Mabinogian;* to England, in Thomas Malory's *Le Morte d'Arthur.* In France, it became the focus of a vast set of chivalric stories known as the *Vulgate Cycle.* Along the way, the romance gave birth to new heroes, including Arthur's knights Lancelot, Galahad and Bors as well as a host of other worthies. The Knights Templars, the militant monks of the Middle Ages whose order flourished as these tales were written, also play a leading role in many Grail stories.

Indeed, although the legend of the Grail quest has not traveled well to cultures beyond Western Europe, it has seldom been out of fashion in France, Germany and Britain. Catnip for the Romantics, the Grail was also a favorite subject for Victorian and Pre-Raphaelite poets and painters. Richard Wagner set the story to music in the opera he regarded as the summit of his art, *Parsifal.* The tale remains popular: Broadway audiences cheer *Spamalot,* a musical version of the 1975 movie send-up *Monty Python and the Holy Grail,* while readers devour Dan Brown's 2003 best seller, *The Da Vinci Code.* In this imaginative thriller, the Grail assumes yet another form, as an ancient, sacred bloodline *(see following story).* And of course, the Grail *is* a kind of ancient bloodline: Chrétien de Troyes, meet Dan Brown.

# In Leonardo's Labyrinth

Watch your back, Arthur Conan Doyle! Dan Brown's 2003 thriller, *The Da Vinci Code*, is a publishing phenomenon rivaling the British master's Sherlock Holmes stories, with 40 million copies in print in hardcover alone. The novel takes readers on a brisk journey through some of the more arcane corners of religion, art and history, and Brown is a splendid tour guide, brewing up a crackling page turner from an unlikely mixture of ingredients: Gnostic gospels, Leonardo da Vinci paintings, biblical exegesis, Roman Catholic fringe groups, pagan fertility rites, secret societies, French kings, English churches, Scottish chapels, nifty secret codes ... and the list goes on.

Perhaps Brown's most significant invention is his central character, Robert Langdon, introduced in Brown's 2000 novel, *Angels and Demons*. The fictional Harvard symbologist — equal parts Philip Marlowe, Indiana Jones and Harold Bloom — is the prism through which Brown refracts a vast amount of research and transforms a by-the-numbers plot into an enjoyable intellectual challenge. Brown himself, it seems, is not unlike Langdon; he is the medium for the research done by his wife Blythe. This point emerged after Brown's publisher was sued in Britain in 2006 by two writers who claimed he had appropriated the basic architecture of his book from their 1982

*The Da Vinci Code* mixes a cops-and-robbers plot with a seminar on the history of art and religion. Here are a few of the clues pursued by Robert Langdon and his foes in the story:

**LOUVRE MUSEUM** The glass pyramid designed by I.M. Pei, completed in 1989, is the alpha and omega of the plot

**THE LAST SUPPER** The novel claims that the figure on the left in Da Vinci's famed fresco is not the Apostle John, but rather Mary Magdalene, Christ's wife

**VITRUVIAN MAN** Da Vinci's sketch is the template for the message left by the slain Louvre curator Jacques Saunière

**SAINT-SULPICE** The Paris church has a meridian line set into its floor

**MARY MAGDALENE** Christ's disciple holds a chalice in this unattributed 16th century painting from the Netherlands

nonfiction work, *Holy Blood, Holy Grail.* They lost the case.

From the origin of the compass rose on maps to the number of panes in I.M. Pei's glass pyramid at the Louvre (which Brown fibs about), readers of *The Da Vinci Code* come away with a little learning about many important issues — and that can be a dangerous thing. So let's get right to what most readers really want to know about the novel: How much of this stuff is true? (Spoiler alert: we'll explore details of the plot along the way, so if you're one of the 10 or 12 people who still haven't read the book or seen the movie, beware!)

It's fair to say that many of the facts cited by Brown in the book are

accurate: yes, Leonardo da Vinci kept notebooks written in a secret code (and yes, Bill Gates did purchase one of the most famous of them). Yes, Brown's descriptions of the Louvre, Rosslyn Chapel in Scotland, Saint-Sulpice Church in Paris and Winchester Cathedral in London are accurate. Yes, the Roman Catholic Church suppressed ancient pagan religions centered on maternal figures in the first centuries after Christ. (Although Brown stretches this point a bit; the early church often chose to adopt some of the rites and figures of pagan religions into church doctrine, rather than suppress them — hence our Maypole, Christmas tree and many other once pagan religious symbols.) Yes, Opus Dei is a right-wing Catholic organization, some of whose members practice mortification of the flesh. Yes, any number of alternate Gospels were not included when the official Roman Catholic version of the New Testament was first drawn up. Only a month before the premier of the film version of Brown's book, scholars released the text of one such Gnostic work, the 1,700-year-old *Gospel of Judas,* an apocryphal Gospel in which Judas is a collaborator in Christ's plans, rather than his betrayer.

Brown takes most of his liberties in the plot devices that drive his thriller — what Alfred Hitchcock used to call "the MacGuffin." One MacGuffin is the Holy Grail, which, Langdon informs us, is not the chalice used by Christ at the Last Supper but is rather a bloodline. Jesus Christ, it seems, married Mary Magdalene and produced a dynasty of heirs that survives to this day. The antimatriarchal early church, determined to suppress the sacred dynasty, painted Mary Magdalene as a prostitute and suppressed knowledge of the Grail bloodline, which was later absorbed into the Merovingian line of French kings. This secret has been passed down through history by a secret society of illuminati, the Priory of Sion, whose leaders have included Da Vinci, Isaac Newton and Victor Hugo.

Can this be true? Well, no. Respected scholars such as Elaine Pagels of Princeton University have clarified the conflicts in the early church over the role of women in Christianity, conflicts that still persist. But there is not one ancient text that advances the notion that Mary Magdalene married Jesus Christ, or bore his child, or claims that such a bloodline still exists. Moreover, the argument that Mary Magdalene was not a prostitute steals the meaning from her story — Christ's embrace of those lowest on the social ladder and shunning of those on the top rungs is surely at the heart of his teachings.

And then there's the Priory of Sion — or is there? This group, a devout, far-flung, potent cabal in Brown's tale, in reality is neither holy, roamin', nor an empire. A sect of this name was indeed formed in France in the 1950s, but its leader, Pierre Plantard, admitted in the 1980s that its claims to ancient glory were fabrications. Both *Holy Blood, Holy Grail* and *The Da Vinci Code* portray these bogus claims as true, although it's clear that for Brown the priory is just another MacGuffin. As for readers who find the notion that Christ sired a child deeply offensive, it's worth keeping in mind that Dan Brown's job is to sell books rather than write doctrine, and he's doing pretty well at it.

# Petitions and Apparitions

Miracles and visions that seem to transcend nature's laws — and pilgrimages to the places where they are said to have occurred — are central to many of the world's great religions. An obsession with such supernatural events and relics helped ensure the long primacy of the Roman Catholic Church in Europe; abuses of them ushered in the Reformation. Yet the inspirational power of miracles lives on

**PILGRIMS:** A journey of devotion to a sacred site is one of the most ancient rites of organized religion. The completion during one's lifetime of the hajj, a pilgrimage to Mecca, is one of the principal duties of Muslims. The medieval Catholic pilgrims who visited the site of St. Thomas à Becket's murder at Canterbury Cathedral, right, were immortalized in Chaucer's *Canterbury Tales,* as illustrated below. The spirit of pilgrimage is still very much alive in Europe, where the faithful follow the "Way of St. James" to Spain's Santiago de Compostela Cathedral or visit the Jasna Gora monastery in Poland to view icons associated with Christ's disciples.

**BLACK MADONNA OF CZESTOCHOWA:** Pilgrims from around the world join Poles in revering this ancient icon of the Virgin Mary and the Christ child, which legend (almost certainly apocryphal) holds was painted by St. Luke on a tabletop from the home of the Holy Family. The icon is said to have halted the advance of a Swedish army on the monastery of Jasna Gora in 1656, where it still resides.

**MODERN SAINTS?** Pope John Paul II was a firm believer in the inspirational power of sainthood; he named 482 saints during his tenure, far more than any other modern Pope. The church follows strict procedures before it names a person a saint; candidates for canonization are examined in a series of demanding inquries into their life and works, and two posthumous miracles must be attributed to a person's intervention before canonization is declared.

John Paul put the widely respected nun Mother Teresa of Calcutta on a fast track to sainthood after her death, accelerating the usual long timetable of the process. Soon after John Paul's death, his successor, Benedict XVI, put his predecessor on a similar speedy timetable for canonization.

**OUR LADY OF GUADALUPE:** Mexican Catholics venerate an icon of Mary said to have been imprinted on a cloak during her apparition to a peasant, Juan Diego Cuauhtlatoatzin, in 1531. The tale's authenticity cannot be proved, but it made Mexico a Catholic nation. A unifying symbol for Mexicans, the image has been adopted by champions of the nation's indigent for centuries; above, the image is borne in a procession at the Basilica of Guadalupe in Mexico City.

**INCORRUPT?** Sainthood in the Catholic Church is intended primarily to provide inspirational role models for the faithful, but the good works attributed to saints in this world are said to continue into the next, and evidence of the posthumous intercession of saints in the form of visions or miracles of healing is integral to the church's canonization process.

A miracle associated with some saints is the inexplicable incorruptibility of their body after death, said to have occurred to participants in two modern cases treated in this book, the visions at Fatima in Portugal and the apparition of the Virgin Mary at Lourdes, France. The body of St. Bernadette, the visionary of Lourdes, above, is displayed at the basilica.

# Marks of Faith

"We know the mind and body are inseparable," says Mario Martinez. "And stigmata"—the mystical phenomenon by which the faithful can develop wounds that mimic those Jesus Christ endured during crucifixion—"are ideal for studying that." Martinez is a Cuban-born clinical psychologist, now based in Nashville, Tenn., where he founded the Institute of Biocognitive Psychology in 1998 to study, among other things, the little-understood connection between faith and health. "This is one of the most intriguing examples of how biology can transcend its own limits at the service of spiritual beliefs," he explains. "There are studies that show that feelings of compassion can have a positive effect on the immune system. Other studies show the same about confession. Genuine stigmata are cases of individuals extending their powers of mind and body. The mind has power that faith enhances."

Martinez has been called upon more than 20 times by Roman Catholic bishops in the U.S., the Caribbean and Europe to investigate alleged instances of stigmata. "It usually turns out to be self-mutilation or something else science can explain," Martinez says. But in the rarest of instances, Martinez and other investigators are unable to find any worldly basis for what they are seeing. Even then, Martinez doesn't pronounce what he is seeing a miracle. "My job is to rule things out," he says. "That's the role of a scientist."

Martinez's skeptical approach suits church authorities, who are profoundly ambivalent about stigmata, just fine. "They don't want to encourage people to hurt themselves," Martinez explains, "which is what reports of stigmata usually turn out to be." Perhaps that is why the Catholic Church refuses to consider even the most credible reports of stigmata when weighing a candidate for sainthood and similarly will not endorse even the most widely accepted accounts of this type of alleged miracle. Instead the church deems cases of stigmata that science cannot discount to be open to "individual interpretation." However, Vatican teaching does acknowledge at least the potential legitimacy of stigmata, describing those who bear Christ's wounds as people singled out by God "to be united more closely with the sufferings of His Son, souls who are willing in a peculiarly fitting way to expiate the sins of others."

The first recorded case of Christ's wounds appearing on one of his followers came in 1224, when St. Francis of Assisi is said to have begun bleeding from his palms, feet and the right side of his chest. Like most stigmatics, St. Francis was initially accused by church elders of imagining things. Since then, more than 300 alleged cases of stigmata have been reported, with fewer than 50 of them meeting church criteria for being "medically unexplainable." Most cases of stigmata are reported in women, and many alleged stigmatics are nuns. Interestingly, after historical evidence surfaced to indicate that people crucified with nails were impaled through the wrists, rather than the palms (where the bone structure would not support the weight of a suspended human body), subsequent accounts of stigmata reported bleeding from the wrist. Among the signs that church investigators look for: people who bleed for extended periods of time (often months or years) but do not suffer anemia or other ill effects from blood loss, and people who do not develop any infection from the open wounds.

The most recent candidate who appeared to meet both criteria was Francesco Forgione, also called Padre Pio, the Italian Capuchin friar who was canonized in 2002. The mystic is said to have shed as much as one cup of blood daily for the last 50 years of his life. True to form, while the Vatican rigorously investigated miracles attributed to Pio both during his lifetime and afterward as it weighed his case for sainthood, it ignored his alleged stigmata. Indeed, while most varieties of reported miracles are investigated by the Vatican, Rome leaves stigmata to local bishops, who often call upon Martinez.

For his part, the doctor stands stubbornly with one foot planted in the world of science and the other in the world of faith. "I believe in miracles," Martinez explains, "but I also believe that the real miracle is the ability that we have, through the power of belief, to impose upon biology." That has profound implications not only for religion but also for science, Martinez insists: "If you can find out how the mind wounds the body, then it's also possible to learn how the mind can heal the body."

STIGMATICS Padre Pio is on the opposite page. The first reported case of stigmata was that of St. Francis of Assisi, far left, who embraced a life of poverty, self-denial and mortification (he once begged forgiveness of his body, "Brother Ass," for the harsh way his spirit had treated it). Francis first received the stigmata in 1224, at age 43; he died two years later.
Renowned medieval stigmatic St. Catherine of Siena, near left, lived about 100 years after Francis. The mystic received the stigmata and prayed to have the marks removed but still experienced pain.
At right is Bertha Mrazek, a.k.a. Georges Marasco. The dual-personality 20th century Belgian also experienced the stigmata; her bizarre case, perhaps faked or of pathological origin, is an example of why the Catholic church refrains from endorsing stigmatics.

# Bernadette's Healing Spring

Like the nun, pardoner, knight and Wife of Bath in Chaucer's *Canterbury Tales,* modern-day Roman Catholic pilgrims flock to a small town in the remote Pyrenees of western France to bathe in the healing waters of a miraculous spring at Lourdes. It is one of the world's foremost pilgrimage sites: more than 200 million visitors have come here since an impoverished farm girl first reported she had experienced visions of the Virgin Mary in a local grotto. Many of them join the magnificent, moving processions to the grotto and the nearby basilica, where walls bear the crutches of the halt and lame who attest they have been cured here.

The story of Lourdes is the story of Bernadette Soubirous, the oldest of six children from an impoverished family. On Feb. 11, 1858, while gathering firewood near the Grotto of Massabielle, she experienced the first of 18 apparitions of a "beautiful lady" who initially refused to divulge her identity. Although the girl was often accompanied during her visions, no other witnesses shared them. During the ninth vision, the lady commanded Bernadette to drink from the "spring" in the grotto, although no water flowed at the site. According to the legend, the girl dug into the dirt and located a spring, whose healing waters have flowed ever since.

During the 16th vision, Bernadette was holding a candle, which burned near her skin for 15 minutes; a doctor who was present certified that she had no received no injury from its flame. Eventually the lady revealed her identity to the girl. "I am the Immaculate Concep-tion," she reportedly said. Widely known church doctrine today, this term, which means that Mary was born without original sin, was only four years old at the time, and the use of such a technical term by an illiterate peasant girl is a striking aspect of the tale. The Lady urged that a shrine to the Virgin be built on the site and that processions be made to it. A church was built in 1862, followed by a magnificent basilica in 1876. Bernadette never saw the basilica; badly ailing for much of her life, she became a nun in 1866 and died in 1879, at only 35. She was named a saint by the church in 1933.

Stories of medical miracles conferred by the healing waters of the spring closely followed the visions; they have slowed in recent decades but never stopped. Some claim the number of miracles is in the thousands, but cautious leaders of the Roman Catholic Church have verified as "inexplicable" only 66 of the incidents.

The miracles at Lourdes are open to question; professional skeptic James Randi calls the pilgrimage site a "a very successful commercial venture." Some have attempted to explain Bernadette's supernatural visions by natural science, but those efforts seem forced at best; in such cases, one is either a believer or not a believer.

One pilgrim who had no doubts about Bernadette's visions was Pope John Paul II, a product of the Polish church, which retains a strong belief in the miraculous. Visiting Lourdes for the second time as Pope in August 2004, the 84-year-old Pontiff said to his fellow pilgrims, "With you I share a time of life marked by physical suffering, yet not for that reason any less fruitful in God's wondrous plan." It was to be the final journey of John Paul's many travels; eight months later he died in Vatican City.

**PILGRIM** Pope John Paul II visited Lourdes twice during his papacy, in 1983 and in 2004; the picture at left is from the first visit, two years after the attempt on his life in Rome. Above, candle-lit conveyances in procession

# Fatima and the Future

Readers of Portugal's newspaper *O Século* must have been surprised in mid-October, 1917. The paper's editorial stand generally opposed the nation's largest religion, Roman Catholicism, and in recent weeks its editors had trained a skeptical eye on the goings-on near the town of Fatima. Three schoolchildren here had claimed to see an apparition of the Virgin Mary each month since May, always on the 13th day of the month. As news of the visions spread, larger and larger crowds had followed the children to the fields outside the village of Aljustrel each month, but no one other than the youngsters ever saw the visions.

On Oct. 13 some 70,000 people gathered in the fields, lured by the children's report that the apparition had promised a miracle would take place that day. As *O Século* now told its readers, an extraordinary event had indeed taken place: "Before the astonished eyes of the crowd, whose aspect was biblical as they stood bare-headed, eagerly searching the sky, the sun trembled, made sudden incredible movements outside all cosmic laws—the sun 'danced.'"

Other newspapers agreed: *Ordem* reported that the sun "seemed to be in an exceeding fast and whirling movement." Lisbon's *O Dia,* another anticlerical paper, said, "The silver sun … was seen to whirl and turn in the circle of broken clouds."

Outside Portugal, observatories around the world did not record anomalies in the sun's behavior at the time. Yet when skeptics join 70,000 faithful in witnessing unexplained phenomena … something unusual has occurred. In the nine decades since the "miracle of the sun," no one has offered a convincing explanation for the events of Oct. 13, 1917. Scientists have proposed various theories for what the crowd saw: perhaps it was a sundog, a rainbow refraction of the sun's rays on clouds. Perhaps it was a sandstorm from the Sahara, playing tricks with the eyes of the crowd. Perhaps it was simply a mass hallucination, brought on by the fervor of the huge crowd itself—although as a general rule, nonbelievers generally don't make the same observations as believers in such situations. Even commentators who suggest that whatever event took place was an entirely natural phenomenon are confounded by the clear prediction that such an event would occur at just this time and place.

In 1930 the church declared both the "miracle of the sun" and the appearances of the Virgin Mary to the children as "worthy of belief," meaning Catholics may choose to believe in them but are not required to. The three children—Lúcia Santos, 10, and her cousins Jacinta and Francisco Marto, 7 and 8—claimed they first witnessed the apparitions of an angel in 1916. The Virgin Mary first appeared to them on May 13, 1917. The children also claimed that the apparition granted them three visions. Lúcia, who became a nun, described the first two in a 1941 memoir: the first was a vision of hell. The second urged that the world increase its devotion to Mary, and warned of the potential harm to come from Russia (the Bolshevik Revolution occurred two years later). The first two secrets were revealed to the world in 1942; the third was kept under wraps until 2000, when Pope John Paul II ordered it to be released. In Sister Lúcia's account, it is a ghastly vision of the end times of the world, including a reference to a white-robed Pope under fire. Many have chosen to interpret this vision as a reference to the 1981 assassination attempt on John Paul in St. Peter's Square in Vatican City. That event took place on May 13, the anniversary date of the first apparition of the Virgin at Fatima.

Sister Lúcia died on Feb. 13, 2005, at age 97. In 1941 she revealed that in 1917 the apparition promised that Jacinta and Francisco would be taken to heaven soon. Both died in the great influenza pandemic of 1918-19. Exhumed twice, in 1935 and in 1951, Jacinta's body was reportedly found to be incorrupt.

VISIONS Above, Lúcia Santos, right, and cousins Jacinta and Francisco Marto claimed to have seen the Virgin Mary at Fatima. The Marto children died soon after seeing the apparitions; Lúcia became a nun and lived until 2005. The three secrets the children were given are often interpreted as referring to such events as the rise and fall of Soviet Russia, the carnage of World War II and the attempted murder of Pope John Paul II

# Miracles Among Us?

The Middle Ages were the great era of miracles, but a fundamentalist religious tide that began sweeping across the globe in the latter half of the 20th century has put apparitions and visions back on the front pages of newspapers. Often such events seem to reflect cultural attitudes as much as religious ones, and in many cases church authorities avoid endorsing them

**ITALY:** An Italian police officer wipes a statue of 20 century mystic Padre Pio in March 2002, in Messina, Sicily, after witnesses claimed the image shed tears of blood. Reports of weeping statues are not unusual in Italy. Padre Pio was canonized by Pope John Paul II later that year

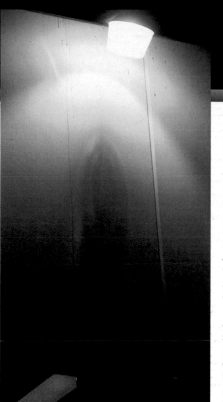

**MEXICO:** Crowds gathered nightly in 2004 in the resort town of Ensenada to see an image resembling the Virgin of Guadalupe, the nation's most revered religious symbol, appear under a patio lamp at a state-run hospital. As the fervor spread, Roman Catholic Church officials stepped in and ruled out a divine origin for the image.

The church is understandably reluctant to endorse such visions: the notorious 2004 eBay sale of a grilled-cheese sandwich said to bear an image of the Virgin (price: $28,000) cheapens authentic religious devotion.

**CALIFORNIA:** A statue of the Virgin Mary in front of the Vietnamese Catholic Martyrs Church in Sacramento showed red stains running from the left eye in 2005. The stains appeared on Nov. 9; fearing a prank, church officials wiped them away. The stains reappeared ten days later. Washed away by New Year's Day rains, the marks have not returned in 2006. Church officials refused to call the incidents miracles and said no investigation into them would be made.

**LONDON:** Reports of alleged miracles swept the globe on Sept. 21, 1995, as countless witnesses claimed to see statues of Hindu deities drinking milk offered with spoons. The tales began in a Delhi temple; soon milk was also said to vanish in Hindu shrines in the U.S. and Europe, above. Skeptical journalists were eyewitnesses in many cases; they had no explanation. Some scientists suggested that plaster statues absorbed the fluid in the process known as capillary action, yet metal statues were also involved. By the next day the strange events were no longer observed in most places.

**AUSTRALIA:** A statue of the Virgin Mary, a picture of Jesus and a crucifix were seen to weep oil or blood at a Vietnamese Catholic center near Brisbane; this picture was taken on May 27, 2004.

An investigation by the church declared that the incidents were little more than a hoax; the red substance found on the crucifix was not blood; the rose-scented oil on others was available commercially; and holes of small diameter had been drilled into the statue and crucifix, through which liquid could be poured.

Long Island, N.Y.

Arkansas

Nepal

# A Prescription for Prayer

Quick quiz: what is the form of alternative-healing therapy embraced by the largest number of Americans ? If you guessed herbal remedies, yoga or acupuncture, your answer is reasonable— but wrong. Prayer comes in first. A 1996 study by the National Institutes of Health found that 43% of Americans pray for their own health, while 24% have others pray for them. A TIME/CNN poll taken the same year showed that 82% of Americans believe prayer can heal. Around the globe, millions more join them, of all faiths.

It's easy to quantify how many Americans are asking for God's help

but determining the effect of their petitions is another matter. One attempt: a 1988 project at San Francisco General Hospital directed by cardiologist Randolph Byrd studied 393 patients in the coronary-care unit. Half, chosen at random,were prayed for by born-again Christians. To eliminate the placebo effect, the patients were not told of the experiment. Remarkably, Byrd found that the control group was five times as likely to need antibiotics and three times as likely to develop complications as those who were prayed for.

A 1999 a study at St. Luke's Hospital in Kansas City, Mo., reached

West Virginia

New Orleans    Macau, China

New Orleans

similar conclusions, reporting that coronary-care patients who were prayed for by Christian groups fared better than patients with no assigned petitioners.

Yet in 2006 the results of the most extensive study ever conducted on the subject found prayers by others (intercessionary prayers) offered no discernible benefit to patients. The study was led by Dr. Herbert Benson, a cardiologist and director of the Mind/Body Medical Institute near Boston. Monitoring 1,802 patients at six hospitals who received coronary bypass surgery, researchers not only found no positive effects among those prayed for, but also concluded that patients who knew they were being prayed for had a higher rate of post-operative complications like abnormal heart rhythms, perhaps because of the expectations the prayers created.

On the larger question of whether faith can aid health, a 1995 study at Dartmouth-Hitchcock Medical Center in New Hampshire found that one of the best predictors of survival among 232 heart-surgery patients is the degree to which the patients said they drew comfort and strength from religious faith. Those who did not had more than three times the death rate of those who did. The following year, a National Institute on Aging study of 4,000 elderly people living at home in North Carolina found that those who attended

religious services were less depressed and physically healthier than those who didn't attend or worshipped at home.

Some of these results may blur the line between correlation and causation. Churchgoers are more apt than nonattendees to respect religious injunctions against drinking, drug abuse, smoking and other vices, so their better health may simply reflect healthier habits.

Even the most encouraging results, however, are inconclusive — as they must be. Part of the problem with asking science to bless prayer is asking prayer to submit to the rigorous quantification of science. That's a challenge. While doctors can monitor dosage levels of a medication they are testing, for example, what constitutes a "dose" of prayer? While control groups can be given sugar pills instead of the medication being tested, how is it possible to be sure that nobody is praying for these patients? Other questions are more theological than medical: Does individual prayer work better than group prayer? Are the prayers of one religion more effective than another?

"Prayer can be and is helpful," says the Rev. Raymond J. Lawrence, director of pastoral care at New York Presbyterian Hospital. "But to think that you can research it is inconceivable to me. Prayer is presumably a way of addressing God, and there's no way to scientifically test God. God is not subject to scientific research."

# The Hands That Heal

Take it as a sign that the world has become more wicked or as an indication that human beings are growing more enlightened, but these are not the best of times for faith healers. Even though more than three-quarters of Americans say they believe God sometimes intervenes to cure illness, and even though physicians and scientists are continuing to explore reported links between religious belief and health, faith healers have suffered from years of

bad publicity. These healers—in the U.S., they are typically evangelical Christian preachers who produce seeming medical miracles by a biblically inspired laying on of hands—are increasingly relegated to the fringes of religious experience.

That may in part be because of the over-the-top claims and deeds of the nation's most prominent healers, which often make people of quieter devotion wince. In 1987 Oral Roberts, the charismatic

Hinn, was born in Israel and educated in Canada. Now based in Texas, he was raised in the Greek Orthodox faith before becoming a powerful Pentecostalist minister. In 1999 the evangelist suggested that viewers might resurrect dead loved ones by basking their corpses in the life-giving glow of TVs tuned to his Trinity Broadcasting Network. Exposés by the Canadian Broadcasting Corporation, NBC News and a number of newspapers have aired allegations of financial impropriety by one of Hinn's former associates and cast a dim light on some of his alleged healings. In the summer of 2005 Hinn acknowledged that the IRS was investigating his operation.

Both the Hinn and Roberts organizations refused to speak with TIME as this book was in preparation. That's not surprising: mainstream media in the U.S., never too comfortable reporting on Fundamentalist Christianity, often portray all faith healers as con men waiting to be unmasked. Yet a number of widely esteemed religious leaders, including Pope John Paul II and the Rev. Billy Graham, have stated their belief that faith healing is a real (if rare) occurrence, although few claim such power for themselves.

Others do make such claims. Dr. Issam Nemeh, a Cleveland, Ohio, physician and acupuncturist, conducts healing ceremonies that draw thousands of sick people and sometimes produce reports of scientifically inexplicable cures. Recent years have also seen a spate of "dental cures" (reports that cavity fillings made with other materials have miraculously been transformed into gold) in California, Florida and elsewhere.

Rationalists dismiss most of these claims as wishful thinking, if not outright lies. In their view, the few healing events that remain scientifically inexplicable are due to the "placebo effect," a medical phenomenon in which the patient's belief in a cure translates into actual improvement. Yet one needn't be a linguist to note that one man's placebo effect is another man's authentic miracle of healing, dressed up in more white-lab-coat terminology.

But perhaps skeptics who want to dissect the magic and believers who wish to document it are both missing the point. Danish philosopher Soren Kierkegaard once wrote that faith doesn't come from miracles—miracles come from faith. Because no reasonable observer could think that the faith of people who turn to healers for help is anything other than passionate, profound and real, perhaps there are forces at work here that transcend science's ability to quantify—or write off as a placebo effect. The connections between the mind, body and spirit, long one of the great unexplored domains of science, are beginning to be charted. As our understanding of these links grow, faith healing may take its place among accepted medical practices—although perhaps under a more New Age name. Spiritual therapy, anyone?

Oklahoma-based Pentecostalist preacher who has been performing faith healings since the 1940s, tested the credulity of his devotees when he announced that he had raised the dead on more than one occasion. A few months earlier, Roberts had warned that God would strike him dead unless his followers sent him $8 million in donations; he took in $9.1 million.

Today's reigning Protestant faith healer, the charismatic Benny

**SHOCK TO THE SPIRIT Evangelist Oral Roberts, seen at left ministering to a patient in the 1960s, became America's most noted faith healer in the 1940s. Roberts, who turned 88 in 2006, presides over a large ministry, including a hospital and university, in Tulsa, Okla.**

**SATAN'S FOE** Father Gabriele Amorth, above, is the Vatican's foremost exorcist (of six). He has performed the ritual since 1986 and claims that there are many different levels of possession. The police department in Rome also maintains a full-time exorcist. At right is Anneliese Michel, who died in 1976 due to gruesome attempts to exorcise her alleged demons; she is the model for the young victim in the film *The Exorcism of Emily* Rose

# Dueling with the Devil

No one doubts there is evil in this world. But it's very much a matter of debate (and belief) as to whether evil is sometimes made manifest in the form of a supernatural personality that seizes control of a human being. What is not open to question is the fact that cases of exorcism—the religious ritual by which such alleged demons are cast out and satanic possession is cured—are on the rise.

The ascendance of evangelical Christianity, with its fervent belief in what exorcism chronicler Malachi Martin called "personal and intelligent evil," along with the Roman Catholic Church's return to traditionalism during the tenure of Pope John Paul II, have led to renewed respect for a rite that had been regarded as arcane by many Christian denominations for much of the 20th century.

Decades of Freudian psychology and medical progress were harsh on exorcism. Conditions previously thought diabolical, such as Tourette's syndrome, proved medically treatable. In the wake of the Second Vatican Council, many American Catholics "wanted to restrict things to only a scientific way of knowing" and shied away from the rite's supernatural literalism, says Father Kazimierz Kowalski, an exorcist in Manhattan. Says Father James LeBar, the former chief exorcist for the Catholic Archdiocese of New York: "The whole thing [belief in demonic possession] kind of went down to embers."

But, says Kowalski, modern culture's lack of a moral anchor and an increasing flirtation with paganism and the occult can lead the susceptible to "put themselves proximate to darkness." That includes non-Catholics. The Rev. Bob Larson, an evangelical minister based in the U.S. who says he conducts hundreds of exorcisms annually, has noticed a significant increase in the past half-decade. The reason? "Moral decay," he says. "The violence, drugs and sex abuse. You don't have to look further than BTK, who says he has demons," Larson explains, referring to the Kansas serial killer who was apprehended in 2005, after a decades-long spree of mutilation murders. Depending on your point of view, the recent increase in exorcisms can be seen to reflect either a greater frequency of demonic possessions or an uptick in incidences of delusion and mental illness masquerading as satanic possession.

For those who believe, there is no confusion. John Paul II is known to have performed at least three exorcisms during his tenure (in

1978, 1982 and 2000), and the New Testament tells of Jesus casting out demons on six occasions. Sober observers are on record as having witnessed phenomena that medical science would be hard pressed to explain. LeBar (who is also the chaplain at a psychiatric hospital) is well aware of the danger of mistaking psychological symptoms for spiritual ones. He calls in a psychiatrist and medical doctor before any exorcism, but, he notes, "there comes a point, when somebody is climbing up the wall or floating on the ceiling or talking a language they've never studied, when it's harder to put it in the 'psychological-problem' bin." In one case of levitation he witnessed, LeBar says, a woman "rose up above pew level and stayed there a little bit and went back down." Less theatrical signs of possession include displays of superhuman strength and an aversion to sacred objects, like holy water and the cross, according to Father Thomas Weinandy, a spokesman for the U.S. Conference of Catholic Bishops.

Exorcists can run afoul of man's law while enforcing God's will. In a real-life case made famous by the 2005 film *The Exorcism of Emily Rose,* German college student Anneliese Michel died in 1976 when her deeply religious parents halted medical treatment for her epilepsy and turned to the Catholic church for help. After enduring twice-weekly exorcisms, during which she refused food and water, for nearly a year, she died of malnutrition. Her parents and the priests involved were convicted of negligent homicide and received six-month suspended sentences. In 2005, an Eastern Orthodox priest and four nuns in Romania were charged with murder after chaining Maricica Irina Cornici, a seemingly possessed 23-year-old woman, to a cross for a three-day exorcism, during which she died.

Despite such horrors, the demand for spiritual rescue continues to rise. Father Gabriele Amorth, the Vatican's chief exorcist—who performs the ceremony more than a dozen times each week and estimates that he has grappled with demons thousands of times—claims to have had glass, keys and nails spat at him. "The objects materialize the instant they come out of the mouth," he says. But Amorth is not daunted by his adversary. "I've never been afraid of the devil," he claims. "In fact, I can say he is often scared of me."

# On Wings of Wonder

As the Civil War drew to an end, Abraham Lincoln summoned Americans to heed "the better angels of our nature." Although often associated with Christianity, these spirits who do heaven's work on earth also appear in the Judaic and Islamic traditions

**GABRIEL:** Christians believe this archangel visited the Virgin Mary to inform her she would bear God's son; as the herald of good news, he is often portrayed with a trumpet. Muslims believe Jibril is the angel who brought the Koran to Muhammad. Art: *The Annunciation*, by Sandro Botticelli, circa 1489.

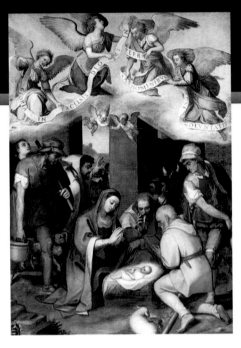

**HEAVENLY CHOIR:** In the *Gospel of Luke,* we read that a herald angel spoke to shepherds on the night of Christ's nativity, saying, "I bring you good news of great joy." A host of angels then appeared, praising the Lord; memories of their voices still resound in Christian churches in the Christmas season. Art: *The Adoration of the Shepherds,* by Marcello Venusti, circa 1550-55.

**RAPHAEL:** This archangel, whose power is healing, plays a minor role in Judaism; in Islam, he will sound the horn on Judgment Day. Roman Catholics know him from the *Book of Tobias* (considered apocryphal by Protestants), in which he appears in human form as Azarias, who travels with Tobias and helps heal his blind father. Art: *Raphael and Tobias,* attributed to Titian, 1507-08.

**MICHAEL:** First among angels in both the Old and New Testaments, this sword-wielding archangel was identified in the *Book of Daniel* as the protector of Israel. Early Christians saw Michael not only as the agent who banished Lucifer from heaven but also as a patron of healing. Art: Michael and Lucifer battle, from a fresco in the Santa Maria di Strada church in San Daniele del Friuli, Italy.

**GUARDIANS:** The idea that each person is assigned a personal guiding spirit, or guardian angel, is powerful, but Roman Catholics may be surprised to learn that it is not an article of faith of their church. Yet St. Jerome wrote, "How great the dignity of the soul, since each one has from his birth an angel commissioned to guard it."

The Greeks spoke of such spirits, but they do not play a large role in Jewish tradition. Speaking of children in the *Gospel of Matthew,* Christ said, "Never despise one of these little ones; I tell you, they have their guardian angels in heaven ..." (New English Bible translation). Art: German holy card.

# A World Beyond

## 6

**❝** It is not you that is mortal, but only your body. For that man whom your outward form reveals is not yourself; the spirit is the true self ... **❞**

— Cicero

# Overtures to the Afterlife?

Owen Thomas died in December 1981. The New York City fish-market worker, 20, was horribly slashed in a knife fight on the Manhattan waterfront, suffering punctures and lacerations to his heart, liver, intestines and one lung. By the time he arrived at the New York Infirmary, he had no pulse, no blood pressure and no breath left in a body that was already "very cold to [the] touch," according to trauma physician Dr. Daryl Isaacs. Yet in a medical miracle that Isaacs later called "the most wondrous thing we've ever experienced," Thomas' heartbeat was restored after vigorous CPR.

When he awoke from more than eight hours of surgery, Thomas described a miracle that had nothing to do with medicine. The normally down-to-earth New Yorker recalled floating into a dark void. "I was going someplace, and then I saw my brother," says Thomas, referring to Christopher Thomas, who had died in a car accident two years earlier. "He put his two big hands on my shoulders and pushed me back, saying, 'You can't come here; there's no room.'"

The gateway from this world to the next—if people who say they've stood at its threshold are to be relied upon—takes many forms. Some recall passing through a blackened tunnel opening into an area of intense, white light that somehow doesn't blind. Others recount ascending a staircase. A third group remembers hovering in mid-air, outside their own bodies, and watching friends and relatives grieve as doctors give up efforts at resuscitation. Variations of these scenarios include being surrounded by animals, meeting departed loved ones, walking through a valley, sailing through an otherworldly blue sky or hearing a disembodied voice— terrifyingly powerful but kind—issue gentle commands.

Such recollections would be easier to dismiss if they weren't so widespread: some studies show that as many as 1 in 5 patients who have been revived from cardiac arrest or other medical states that are the clinical equivalent of death has experienced these visions. Indeed, one of the most intriguing indicators that these memories may be something other than hallucinations is the fact that they occasionally occur in patients who are incapable of hallucinating: a small number of patients register flat brain scans (showing no cerebral activity whatever) before being revived. They could not have imagined the experience of leaving this world, because their brains weren't able to imagine anything while they were so close to death. Nonetheless, these patients sometimes recall in vivid detail having taken a journey into what sounds very much like the afterlife—or its immediate prelude.

We might expect such extraordinary incidents to occur most often in people of deep faith, but that appears not to be the case. A nationwide Gallup poll conducted the year after Thomas' near death experience (NDE) found no correlation between religious devotion or cultural background and the likelihood of paranormal visions during severe medical trauma. In short, an atheist is as likely as a Methodist to experience an NDE. Even young children, who have presumably had less time to absorb the cultural influences that might arguably drive such visions, sometimes report detailed visions of their experiences while being resuscitated.

The same survey, which indicated that more than 8 million Americans have undergone a near death experience, found that many describe the state as "ecstatic," and some find the experience so transfixing that they are unhappy about returning to life. "Why did you bring me back, Doctor?" said one patient. "It was so beautiful!"

While mystical glimpses of the next world are as old as recorded history, interest in exploring such visions within a medical context surged after the 1969 publication of *On Death and Dying* by Elizabeth Kübler-Ross and 1975's *Life After Life* by Dr. Raymond Moody, who coined the term near death experience. His research, which reviewed 150 cases of clinically dead patients who were later revived, documented elements common to almost all NDEs: a feeling of serenity, a sense of floating out of one's body, a journey through a dark passageway toward a warm light, encounters with a supernatural presence and a meeting with dead relatives.

Skeptics point out that one needn't flirt with death to experience such visions: similar dream states can be induced in people suffering from epilepsy by electrically stimulating specific locations in the brain. They are also common among test pilots who undergo cerebral hypoxia—oxygen deprivation in the brain as a result of reduced blood flow during rapid acceleration of an aircraft. And of course, NDEs may represent a transition stage between life and death, not one's final destination. Still, while skeptics and believers argue over proof, a poet might view beautiful visions at the end of life as nature's final gift—the spirit soaring while the body is failing.

**FIAT LUX! Many patients who have clinically died recall visions of a journey through a dark tunnel to an open area brimming with light**

# You've Got Mail!

Although the belief that human consciousness survives death is probably as old as, well, human consciousness, the notion that the living can converse with the dead is of surprisingly recent vintage. It dates to 1848 and got its start in the suburbs of Rochester, N.Y. In the spring of that year, the three teenage daughters of black-smith John Fox claimed to be hearing mysterious rapping noises in their home, a building that had been rumored for years to be haunted. Convinced that a ghost was trying to communicate with them, the sisters developed an alphabet similar to Morse code, in which specific numbers of raps corresponded to various letters. In

this way, the girls quizzed their invisible companion, who identified himself as a murdered peddler whose remains were buried in their basement. When local authorities went digging in the cellar, they found several fragments of bone that appeared to he human. Although that was far from proof positive, the sisters Fox—Maggie, Katie and Leah—quickly found both fame and fortune in communing with spirits. P.T. Barnum sponsored their first national tour, and famed newspaper editor Horace Greeley took them under his wing.

Within a decade, the "séance" (from the Old French word meaning "to sit") had become part of mainstream culture, with spiritualists (or

Queen Victoria entered a decades-long period of mourning after her consort, Prince Albert, died in 1861.

In the Edwardian age, English spiritualists were led by Arthur Conan Doyle. Ironically, the creator of fiction's foremost rationalist, Sherlock Holmes, became a passionate believer in the spirit world. In later years, the desire to establish contact with lost loved ones was made more urgent by the carnage of World War I, in which Doyle lost a brother and a son and Britain lost a generation of young men.

It was Doyle's close friend Harry Houdini, the leading magician of the age, who eventually helped kill the séance craze. Playing a role similar to the one filled today by Penn & Teller or James Randi, Houdini debunked unscrupulous spiritualists, exposing the stage tricks used to create such startling effects as moving furniture and mysterious noises. Instantly recognized by the public and feared by mediums, Houdini often resorted to attending séances in disguise, sometimes with an undercover police officer in tow, to make arrests for fraud. After Houdini publicly proclaimed himself still unconvinced following a 1922 séance in Atlantic City, N.J., which was presided over by Doyle's wife Jean, the two men ended their long friendship.

Within four years, Houdini was dead. But he had one last trick to play. Boasting that "if anybody could escape from the beyond, it would be me," the magician and his wife Bess agreed that she would try to contact him after he died. To prevent trickery, they agreed on an unbreakable code: 10 words selected randomly from one of Doyle's books. True to her word, Bess convened a séance each year on the anniversary of Houdini's death—Halloween night. For 10 consecutive years, various mediums claimed to be channeling her husband's ghost, but not one of them could divine the words they had agreed upon. Finally, Bess announced that "10 years is long enough to wait for any man" and gave up. Today, séances are often held in Houdini's honor on Oct. 31, but they are mostly regarded as a nostalgic joke—which is in fact how this once popular parlor pastime is now generally regarded.

And what of the women who started it all? In later life, the Fox sisters developed serious drinking problems, struggled with emotional instability and underwent religious conversions; as a result, they came to regard their earlier careers as diabolical. In the 1890s they confessed to having made up their accounts of speaking to the dead; later they declared that confession was a lie. Even as spiritualism was still the rage, all three sisters died before the turn of the century, penniless and forgotten. So almost nobody took notice in 1904—11 years after the last surviving Fox sister had died and more than 50 years after they first claimed to hear from the spirit world—when a complete human skeleton was found buried in the walls of their childhood home in Rochester.

It is hard not to imagine that, somewhere, both Harry Houdini and Arthur Conan Doyle are smiling about that one. If you hear from them, let us know.

mediums) entering trances to speak to—and on behalf of—the dead. The public's embrace of spiritualism reached into the White House and across the Atlantic. Abraham Lincoln was convinced by his wife Mary Todd to participate in several sittings to reach their son Willie, who died in 1862 at age 11. The boy didn't appear, but Lincoln got garbled, contradictory words of counsel from George Washington, Benjamin Franklin and Napoleon. He later quipped that "their advice sounds a good deal like the talk of my Cabinet." In Britain, eminent Victorians also became spellbound by the prospect of reaching out to the dearly departed, particularly after death became fetishized when

**NIGHTS OF THE ROUND TABLE A scene from a 1920s film captures the rituals of the séance: hands are poised to feel the vibrations of spirits**

# Spirits of the Dead

On a brilliant day in the spring of 1980, a stranger arrived at L'Estere marketplace in Haiti's fertile Artibonite Valley. The man's gait was heavy, his eyes vacant. The peasants watched fearfully as he approached a local woman named Angelina Narcisse. She listened as he introduced himself, then screamed in horror—and recognition. The man had identified himself with the boyhood nickname of her deceased brother Clairvius Narcisse, a name that was known only to family members and had not been used since his funeral in 1962.

This event, along with others like it, sparked the most systematic inquiry ever undertaken into the legendary voodoo phenomenon of zombiism, the belief that dead bodies can be reanimated by unnatural means. In a paper published a few years later in the *Journal of Ethnopharmacology,* Harvard University scientist Wade Davis concluded that "Zombiism exists and is a societal phenomenon that can be explained logically." At least 15 individuals examined in Davis' study, who had been branded zombies by terrified local peasants, turned out to be victims of epilepsy, mental retardation, insanity or alcoholism. The case of Clairvius Narcisse, however, was harder to decrypt. Medical records showed he was declared dead in 1962 at Albert Schweitzer Hospital, an American-run institution in Deschapelles, Haiti. Yet more than 200 people recognized him after his reappearance. Narcisse said that he had been "killed" by his brothers for refusing to go along with their plan to sell the family land. The best explanation, researchers concluded, was that Narcisse had been poisoned, using herbal toxins that are a specialty of voodoo priests, in such a way that his vital signs could not be detected by the unsophisticated medical instruments used in Haiti at the time. Then his "corpse" had been brought back to life.

This study was part of an ongoing re-examination of voodoo as a whole. Rooted in West African tribal religions, voodoo, which is called vodun in present-day Benin, migrated to the New World with the slave trade. Once ensconced in the Caribbean, it merged with Catholic ritual and belief to form a unique spiritual panoply of saints and spells, curses and cures. Voodoo is particularly associated with the nation of Haiti, but similar amalgams of African folk religions and Christian practices are common in Brazil and across the Caribbean.

Voodoo as seen in Hollywood movies, however, bears little resemblance to folk practices of the Haitian countryside, where a popular saying holds that the nation is "90% Catholic and 110% voodoo." Sticking pins into dolls to induce pain in the people they represent is almost unheard of in real-life voodoo, where dolls (especially those meant to resemble dead friends and relatives) are used to convey messages, written on small scrolls, to the afterlife.

In recent years, voodoo has emerged from the shadows in Haiti, where its practitioners have often been persecuted and sometimes killed. A voodoo priestess was invited to bestow a ceremonial sash on President Jean-Bertrand Aristide during his 1991 inauguration. In 2003 voodoo priests were given official permission to conduct weddings and baptisms. Voodoo even figures in U.S. politics. In November 1998, Florida state senator Alberto Gutman charged his opponent with using voodoo against him in an election. Whatever the merit of his claim, Gutman lost. In 2002 the National Labor

Relations Board was called upon to investigate whether union activists used voodoo to organize employees at a nursing home, also in Florida. The NLRB ruled they had not done so.

Indeed, work and free will are two keys to understanding the dread fascination that zombies hold for the people of Haiti, who are descended from slaves. Wade, whose 1986 book, *The Serpent and the Rainbow,* offers a fascinating introduction to voodoo, explains that "historically, if an individual offended the village's very powerful fetish priests, they would be infected with a poison from the blow-fish, which tends to put you in a comatose-like state of hibernation for a while. Individuals would wake up from it with a certain degree of brain damage, so in a sense, they really were like the walking dead." Afterward, Haitian lore teaches, zombies have no choice but to do the bidding of their new masters, sometimes working in sugar plantations. That is what Clairvius Narcisse claimed to have been doing for almost 20 years between his "death" and reappearance. "Zombies lose their will and become mindless slaves," Wade explains. "Voodoo practitioners aren't afraid of zombies; they are afraid of being turned into zombies."

**RITES Women pray at a voodoo ceremony; participants often believe that they are possessed by spirits. One woman's clothes are blood-stained; like other African folk religions, voodoo features the sacrifice of small animals**

# Major Arteries Open

"Human fascination with blood goes back to the beginning of recorded time," explains Raymond McNally, a history professor at Boston University who has done extensive research on the folklore of vampires. "Primitive man saw that when the blood went out of the body, the life went out. So they naturally assumed that by putting blood back in, you could put the life back in."

Perhaps this is why so many cultures have passed down myths of half-human creatures that cheat death by drinking blood. Aztec mythology told of the *civatateo,* while the ancient Greeks dreaded the *lamia.* In China, the blood drinker is called *jiang-shi,* and people in remote areas of the Philippines fear a creature that bears a chilling resemblance to the vampires of Western popular culture: the *manananggal* not only drinks human blood but also flies on bat wings and is vulnerable to garlic.

Vampire lore is strongest in the Slavic nations of Eastern Europe; just as Eskimos are reported (erroneously) to have more than 30 names for snow, Slavs and Romanians describe many different forms of the undead creature that feeds on the blood of the living. The apparatus of the legend, mostly drawn from this region, has become familiar: the vampire can't be seen in mirrors; shuns garlic, daylight and crucifixes; prefers to sup from the carotid artery; can only be killed by a stake driven through the heart.

Less familiar are some other elements of Slavic lore: the vampire can transform into smoke, straw or dust as well as a bat; cannot enter a home unless invited; avoids rivers and streams; can be killed by decapitation. And as for that bat, its name reflects the legend, rather than the other way around. Blood-eating bats are not indigenous to Europe: they were first discovered in Central and South America by Spanish conquistadors, who named them for the bloodthirsty mythological monster.

The Slavic legends first got hearts pumping in Britain and the U.S. in the form of Dracula, the evil, sleek count dreamed up by British novelist Bram Stoker in his classic 1897 novel. The character was inspired by Vlad III, a Romanian prince of the 15th century, but in this case, the connection between fiction and fact is highly tenuous. A fierce warrior, the prince was also known as Vlad Draculea, which

**MODELS Inset, Vlad the Impaler and the plaque marking his birthplace. At right is Bran Castle; though not inhabited by Vlad, it was used by novelist Bram Stoker as the template for Dracula's castle, where tourists now shed money, if not blood. Coming soon: a $32 million theme park, Dracula Land**

In această casă a locuit
între anii 1431~1435,
domnitorul Țării Românești
VLAD DRACUL,
fiul lui
Mircea cel Bătrîn.

translates loosely as "Son of the Dragon." The Dragons were an order of Christian knights who resisted Islamic expansion into Eastern Europe during the 1400s. Vlad's enemies were Hungary and Turkey, which were constantly at war with each other and Romania during the 15th century. For the deft political balancing and ferocious military force with which he fended off both these aggressors, as well as for founding the capital city of Bucharest, Vlad is still revered as a national hero of Romanians.

Even so, the prince was apparently capable of considerable unpleasantness. His habit of driving wooden stakes into the bodily orifices of his captives earned him the memorable moniker Vlad the Impaler. The lone factual point at which the Vlad of history and Stoker's fictional Dracula seem to intersect is the Impaler's reputation for enjoying a meal as he watched his victims die, occasionally dipping his bread into their blood before eating it.

**CHOMP! The saliva of vampire bats retards blood-clotting in its victims; contrary to myth, the bats lap the blood of their prey rather than suck it**

Today, reports of vampire sightings are rare, even in rural Romania. But the influence of Stoker's imagination remains pervasive—not only in television, film and fiction but also in the lifestyles of self-styled "sanguinarians"—people who drink blood voluntarily given (or sold) to them by human donors.

Very rarely, the line separating eccentricity and insanity is crossed by people obsessed with vampirism. In 1978, California police apprehended Richard Trenton Chase, a serial killer who had become known as "the Sacramento Vampire." In a month-long killing spree, he shot and slashed six people (including a 22-month-old baby), in each case stirring their blood in a kitchen blender before drinking it. When questioned by interrogators, Chase explained that the fluid within his veins was turning to powder, and he needed to replace it with fresh human blood, or else he would die. His career in crime is an unhappy example of fact following fiction.

# Photo Ops for Phantasms

Older than history, ghost stories are told in every culture. Ghosts are generally believed to be the spirits of the departed who remain on earth in incorporeal form, often haunting sites where great psychic energy has been released, perhaps by murder, crime or betrayal. Although most scientists scoff at such tales, everyone loves a good ghost story—or a good ghost picture. Here are some of our favorites

**BACKSEAT DRIVER:** This well-known picture of a spirit was taken by Briton Mabel Chinnery in 1959. After photographing her mother's grave, she took a picture of her husband in their car; when the film was developed, it showed Chinnery's late mother sitting in the backseat. Experts who examined the film stated that they did not think it had been tampered with.

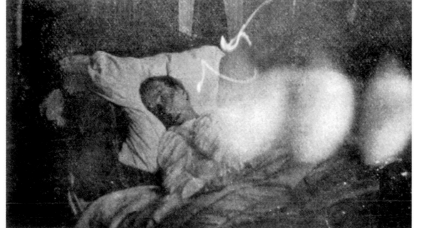

**THE SOUL IN FLIGHT?** French neurologist Hippolyte Baraduc was fascinated by psychic research; eager to capture the body's spiritual energy on film, he photographed the bodies of both his wife and son after their deaths. While his wife lay dying in 1907, Baraduc photographed her as she gave three final gasps, then expired. When the film was developed, three luminous globes were seen hovering over her body; in a later image, the three globes unite into one. Baraduc described psychic energy as "the vital current."

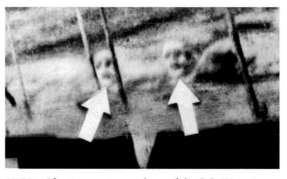

**AT SEA:** After two crew members of the S.S. *Watertown* were killed by a fire and buried at sea in 1924, their fellow mariners said they saw their faces in the water, following the ship. Captain Keith Tracy was moved by the events; he bought a camera and took this picture, which is the least convincing photo on these pages.

**HAUNTED HALL:** This famous picture is said to show the "Brown Lady" who haunts Raynham Hall in Norfolk, England. She is thought to be the spirit of Lady Dorothy Townshend, who may have been mistreated by her husband, owner of the hall. The image was caught on film in 1936 when a magazine photographer's deputy sensed a presence on the stairs and urged him to take a picture, although neither could see anything. The image was revealed when the film was developed.

# Amityville: Hoax or Horror?

The most famous haunted house in America is a lovely Dutch colonial home in a lovely Long Island town with a lovely name: Amityville. There is no doubt that true horrors took place here: on the night of Nov. 13, 1974, Ronald DeFeo Jr., 23, high on heroin and rage, shot and killed his parents and four siblings while they slept. He was convicted of the murders and sentenced to six life terms in prison.

That was the first horror. The second, more famous horror, took place later, when George and Kathy Lutz and their three children moved into the house after the gruesome murders. Within days, they later said, strange events began occurring: slime appeared on the

carpet, strange odors and eerie sounds filled the home. Alarmed, the Lutzes called a priest to bless the house — but the priest was chased away by a strange voice screaming, "Get out!" The events peaked, they claimed, on a horrible night when George Lutz was held captive in his own bed by an unseen force while Kathy levitated above hers and strange noises rocked the children's bedroom. The next morning, only 28 days after they moved in, the Lutzes fled the haunted house.

That's how the story goes, as the Lutzes tell it. And after they told it to writer Jay Anson, he turned it into a 1977 book, *The Amityville Horror*, which became a publishing sensation: to date it has sold

**THE FIRST HORROR** Ronald (Butch) DeFeo Jr. is under arrest, above, on Nov. 15, 1974, two days after he murdered his parents, two brothers and two sisters. He is now serving six life-term sentences in a New York State prison. During his trial he claimed "voices" had told him to commit the murders, but in 2002 he admitted to ABC News that he had concocted that story

**VICTIMS?** Amityville village elders have changed the address of the DeFeo home, left, in hopes of discouraging sightseers. In similar fashion, a later owner removed the quarter-moon windows on the home's third floor, featured heavily in the 1979 film *The Amityville Horror,* and replaced them with more traditional square windows, as seen in this recent photo. The Lutzes, seen above on a 1979 movie promotional tour, later divorced, but continued to insist their story was true. Kathy Lutz died in 2004

some 10 million copies. Hollywood, where the scent of blood often mingles with the scent of money, soon came calling. A 1979 film of the Lutzes' tale made some $80 million at the box office, and a 2005 low-budget remake of the film kept the story in the limelight.

The problem: since Anson's book first appeared, critics have charged that the Lutzes fabricated their tale in hopes of profiting from it, pointing out that the couple received some $300,000 from selling their rights to the story. The most damaging accuser was William Weber, Ronald DeFeo's attorney. After the book appeared, Weber related that he had met with the Lutzes after DeFeo's trial and discussed the notion of inventing the story of the haunted house. In Weber's telling, his wine-fueled brainstorming session with the Lutzes went well, but he later fell out with the couple, who then took

the bogus stories to Anson. The local Roman Catholic diocese refused to confirm the book's account of the priest's experience; he is long dead. Nor does the testimony of several subsequent owners of the home support the Lutzes' tales: none of the later inhabitants have reported paranormal events during the time they lived there.

Some psychics believe the Lutzes' story; one claimed the home was built over—you guessed it—a Native American cemetery, and that Indian spirits had spurred DeFeo's dark deeds as well as the Lutzes' hauntings. Long Island historians say there are no records that the area was ever a burial ground for the local Shinnecock tribe.

Yet the story of the horrors lives on, and those who wish to explore it in further detail have a wonderful opportunity to do so—at the for-profit website owned by George Lutz, *Amityvillehorror.com.*

# Where Ghosts Dwell

Haunted houses? You bet. Not only are certain homes said to be afflicted by spirits, but some of the world's most renowned buildings — including the White House, the Tower of London, Hampton Court Palace and the Theatre Royal on Drury Lane — are said to play host to ghosts, in most cases, several of them. Here is a Baedeker of the Bizarre for would-be ghostbusters

**WHALEY HOUSE:** Built by Thomas Whaley in San Diego in 1857, this is one of the most famous haunted houses in America. Whaley's site selection could have been better: the house sits atop an old public gallows site–and a Native American burial ground. Whaley's son Thomas and daughter Violet died here; Violet shot herself at age 17, but some suspect she may have been murdered. Later, an actor renting an upstairs room stabbed a woman who ran downstairs and died in the garden. Among the weird manifestations of psychic energy said to be witnessed here are strange odors, the sound of footsteps, apparitions of semi-invisible figures and floating orbs of light. A team from ghost-happy website Eeeek-net (www.eeeek.com) concluded the spirits responsible were those of Violet Whaley, her father Thomas and mother Anna. One scaredy-cat: Regis Philbin, who tried to sleep here in 1974 when host of a local TV show. He fled in terror.

**HAMPTON COURT PALACE:** The ghost of Jane Seymour, Henry VIII's third wife, supposedly haunts the huge Renaissance mansion; she died here in 1537. Fifth wife Catherine Howard is said to create a draft in its Haunted Gallery. In October, 2003, security cameras snagged an image of a robed man exiting through a fire door, below. Officials said the image was not a hoax—and could not explain it. "It was incredibly spooky," said James Faulkes, a security guard, "the face just didn't look human."

**TOWER OF LONDON:** The great edifice, constructed in 1078 to ensure William the Conqueror's rule over England, has seen much torture, bloodshed and death. The Duke of Gloucester is believed to have had his two nephews, Princes Edward and Richard, killed here in 1483. As King Richard III he then ascended the throne he had stolen from Edward. Anne Boleyn, Henry VIII's second wife, was beheaded on Tower Green in 1536; her ghost is said to lead a procession of knights and ladies each year on the anniversary of Henry's execution of the Countess of Salisbury in 1541. Sir Thomas à Becket is reputed to haunt a small chapel near Traitor's Gate built in his honor in the 1240s.

**WHITE HOUSE:** The building's ghosts survived a complete renovation ordered by President Harry Truman in the late 1940s. Both the Lincoln Bedroom, below, and the Queen's Bedroom are said to be haunted; the former by Lincoln's ghost, perhaps mourning the death of son Willie, who died in this bed in 1862; the latter by the spirit of boisterous Andrew Jackson, who is said to laugh and swear loudly.

**THEATRE ROYAL, DRURY LANE:** The bewigged gentleman in the tricorn hat (a photographer's fiction) is a stand-in for one of the reputed ghosts of this venerable theater. Known as the "man in grey," this gent, unlike many theater spooks, is a member of the audience, rather than a ghostly performer; he frequents the upper circle. Less elegant is the ghost of actor Charles Macklin, who is lean and mean: Macklin killed fellow actor Thomas Hallam after an argument in 1735. The theater, which opened in 1812, is the fourth on the site.